Web of Lies

Copyright©2024 T.J. Shoults

All Rights Reserved

ISBN: 9798336670769

Dedication

This book is dedicated to my daughters Amanda and Kelsey as well as my wonderful and amazing granddaughter Blake. I would also like to thank my dear wife Maureen for her patience and support during the writing of the book. I love you all!

Web of Lies

Scandal and Lust

At Carlton School

T.J. Shoults

Chapter 1

It was 5:45 A.M. and Lianna woke up in a cold sweat. Her heart pounded like a bass drum beating wildly as she sat straight up in her bed. Breathing heavily, she said to herself, "I'm going to be ok." She'd been having nightmares about work but this one was more intense. Her heart finally slowed down when she realized where she was.

She'd been a school principal for 10 years and loved working with kids. Her colleagues always convinced her to pursue the role, but she was never quite sure about her decision. When she had her own children a few years later, it turned out to be the right one ... or so she thought until just last week when things got crazy.

Tonight, she would face the parent council, and she knew it wasn't going to be an easy meeting. Her school's funding was being cut and she would need to increase fundraising efforts. As schools go however, hers had a wealthy clientele who always stepped up and donated to what they felt were worthy causes that were of great benefit to their kids.

Lianna's worst parent nightmare was a "power broker" parent in the community named Noella De Haviland, who had a powerful influence on many people, not only in the school but also the community at large. Noella had lived in Mount Dorchester for many years and her ex-husband started a major airline in the city that sold for a huge profit.

Both Noella and her husband Collin came from "old money" and they knew how to wield the power and influence that came with it. Noella was known to intimidate people quite easily, and she had also been a city councilor several years back. There was question about her integrity and some said she also had a violent side which ultimately caused her divorce.

Lianna finally got out of bed starting her morning routine reading the paper online and drinking coffee. She used to work out vigorously in the morning but as her daughters got older and became teenagers, she found she had less energy the busier she got.

She prepared a breakfast of eggs on toast, then sat down to watch some news. One of her daughters entered the kitchen and greeted her with a sleepy smile. "Good morning, dear!" said Lianna to her sixteen-year-old daughter Diane. Lianna dearly loved her but, as with all teenagers, there was a bit of tension between them especially when it came to boys and dating.

Lianna knew how to set boundaries without being overbearing and controlling but she still felt an emotional distance that was not there with her younger daughter Dallas who was now 14. Dallas annoyed her sister, acting like a self-proclaimed expert on relationships which especially drove Diane crazy.

"Hey Mom," Diane responded, "what's for breakfast?" Diane knew that her mom didn't really like cooking but did it for them anyway, so she was hopeful that this morning she might get a hot breakfast.

"I'm a bit short of time today, Diane, so you'll have to cook something yourself or grab some cereal. Maybe waffles or toast? I'm so sorry sweetheart but I have meeting with a parent before school and I really have to leave soon.

"I guess I shouldn't be surprised," said Diane who was clearly frustrated with her mother. Diane turned abruptly and stormed out of the kitchen.

"I'm sorry sweetie!" yelled Lianna after her apologetically. Lianna felt the guilt, but at the same time, her daughters were old enough to get themselves breakfast.

Lianna finished tidying up then headed for the door, grabbing her car keys as she quickly passed the counter in the mud room. She hoped it was not going to be one of those days.

****

The parent council gathered in the school library that evening and with a good turnout. Lianna was fully prepared with all her documents from the board office and ready to defend allocating money to more staff.

She spoke passionately to the group, adamantly advocating for another educational assistant to serve the needs of the students. She opened a Q and A which sparked some debate and opposition. Allocating money to staff meant giving up some fine arts equipment, which had been earmarked for purchase by the parents.

"I don't think you realize who you're dealing with here," said Noella with an entitled tone in her voice. "Do you realize the implications of rejecting our request?" she added, sounding threatening as she glared at Lianna.

Lianna stared back at Noella trying not to break eye contact as the two of them squared off. Lianna decided she had no choice but to stand up for the needs of her students at Carlton School.

Noella wanted to commit funds from council for fine arts at the school while Lianna's proposal would better support learning needs.

Noella's proposal was to buy 4 lighting trees with 8 spotlights, a professional lighting board, a new sound system for the gym as well as 6 wireless microphones to be used in dramatic productions.

"And I don't think you realize the impact that an Ed assistant can have on student learning, Noella," Lianna countered, not backing down from Noella's condescending words.

"I'm pleading with council to accept my proposal in light of recent government budget cuts," Lianna implored with passion and determination in her voice.

Noella sat with a frustrated look on her face then glanced over at her *partner in crime* on council, Will Baxter, who also lobbied for the funds. "We have waited far too long for this equipment," exclaimed Will, "and we're not prepared to postpone this purchase any longer!"

The chair of the school council, Maryanne Markham, sat quietly for a moment, then spoke up. "Does anyone else have anything to add about this?" She looked at each person in the room as much as she could. When no one spoke, she said "Then it looks like we need to put this to a vote. What is the motion before us?" she asked the recording secretary Millie, who diligently took minutes at each monthly meeting.

"The motion reads," paused Millie, "that the parent council approve twenty thousand dollars to be used for the purchase of lighting and sound equipment for dramatic productions here at the school." Millie looked very satisfied as she read the motion with clarity and confidence.

"All those in favor?" Maryanne asked and looked around the room for hands. Lianna was hopeful as the seconds passed and no more than three hands went up. "Those opposed?" added Maryanne, now looking intently around to count the votes accurately.

The majority of parents in the room voted against the motion, which visibly frustrated Noella and Will, as the arts equipment would not be purchased.

"I can't believe you are all so naïve!!" cried Noella in frustration. "Do you know how long we've waited for this equipment and now that we have the money, you're all backing out! You're all just a bunch of two-faced back stabbers!" Noella then got up and said, "Come on Will. Let's leave these losers to destroy the school. They deserve it anyway!" Will slowly got up and together they headed down the hall toward the exit.

Maryanne thought quickly as Noella and Will walked away then she called out. "Noella, there must be a compromise or another solution here! Can't we talk about this a little further?"

Maryanne was not the kind of person to see someone leave a meeting angry so she appealed to Noella to stay. "There must be something else we can do to afford the equipment," said Maryanne desperately.

The council members looked at Maryanne then at each other and wondered why she was so intent on pleasing Noella. Was it her financial status which Maryanne found threatening? Was it her social position in the community or was there something else that no one knew about that motivated her to seek Noella's approval so fervently?

They all watched as Noella and Will stormed toward the front foyer of the school. It was obvious Noella didn't want to hear any more. Maryanne asked for a motion to support Lianna's proposal, and soon it was approved.

"Now may I also get a motion to adjourn?" There was no hesitation as many hands went up. She was relieved that this meeting was over as was Lianna, who didn't expect the council to side with her tonight, but got the result she hoped for.

Following the meeting, Maryanne privately asked for Lianna's time. After everyone left the school, Lianna said, "Let's meet in my office. I have a little something in my desk drawer I think we could both use."

Lianna smiled then the two of them walked slowly and silently together. They were both reflecting on what had happened and what Noella's next move might be. They entered Lianna's office which was beautifully decorated.

"Please Maryanne, let's sit at my table. I don't like looking at people across my desk …unless they're in trouble!" she playfully jested. They both laughed and sat down at the round oak table beside Lianna's desk.

"I can't believe the nerve of that woman!" Maryanne began, "She insulted our entire council and questioned our integrity!" Lianna carefully considered what she said to Maryanne next.

"To be honest Maryanne, I was surprised that you didn't shut her down faster. As soon as she started saying things like 'Naïve two-faced backstabbers' … I thought she might get a reprimand from the chair." Lianna was trying to keep this light but Maryanne knew where Lianna was coming from. Neither one was quite sure how to deal with Noella and they sat still for a moment.

"So would you like to have a taste of what's in my drawer?" Lianna asked with a mischievous tone in her voice. "I promise you won't be disappointed." Maryanne waited with anticipation as Lianna opened the drawer. Out came a bottle of Liqueur.

"Well…if you insist," she said with an equally devilish tone.

"Don't worry Maryanne," Lianna replied, "what happens in this office, stays in this office ... Especially peanut butter crème liqueur!"

"You're the best Lianna! Other principals never had anywhere near the quality of liqueur you do," Maryanne confirmed as Lianna poured the liquid into a fancy rock glass.

She knew that Maryanne was stressed out as council chair but no one else was willing to take the job. Maryanne had been elected by acclamation but it had been difficult for her.

"If she didn't have 3 kids in this school," said Maryanne, "I'd be tempted to suggest she go elsewhere." Maryanne took a long sip from her glass. "Ummm...this is delicious," she said as she savored every drop.

Lianna was surprised by Maryanne's comment about Noella, but would never suggest it. Secretly, Lianna wished she herself could tell Noella where to go but she knew her job might be on the line. "It was a good year, I believe." They both laughed as they carefully sipped the nectar.

Lianna responded to Maryanne's reaction to the liqueur. Let's hope the school year is as good as the peanut butter!" They both laughed and soon they were feeling much better about the evening.

"Thanks for this, Lianna," said Maryanne. "I have a feeling this is not the first time we're going to do this after a council meeting!" Lianna chuckled and agreed.

As they set the school's alarm system and walked off toward the parking lot together, Lianna got an eerie feeling that they were not alone.

Chapter 2

Mitch Mason reached out his hand to shake Noella's as she entered his maintenance office door at the school board headquarters. He took a close look at her attire and the huge rings on her fingers and it told him a lot about her. She was, as some would put it, one of the Jason housewives of Mount Dorchester.

Mitch was not hard to look at himself - a guy who went to the gym daily, wore fashionable clothing to the office now that he was no longer a caretaker in the school system. He'd been promoted from the ranks after getting a stellar review every year and as the system needed more leadership, he was a natural fit to supervise others in the maintenance department. But he also had in-depth knowledge of the schools he worked in.

"Hello Mrs. De Haviland" he said. He gazed into her beautiful green eyes and did his best to flirt with her. As they shook hands, Mitch held on just a little longer than he would have when greeting clients. Mitch was divorced, knowing full well Noella was also divorced, and that she had a bad break-up from her ex-husband.

"Hello Mr. Mason," she said with a somewhat flirtatious tone. "Good to see you again." They held eye contact for a few seconds and then Noella asked, "May I sit down, Mr. Mason?"

"Absolutely. I'm sorry Mrs. De Haviland." Mitch responded apologetically. He wondered what she was after and why she was really there. He'd also heard a rumor that she'd challenged several principals before, and that she was no one to mess with.

"It's *Ms.* De Haviland now, but please call me Noella," she stated, again in a flirtatious tone of voice. Mitch was worried for a moment, then quickly moved on to the business at hand.

"What can I do for you today, Noella," Mitch asked, trying not to sound flirtatious.

"Well … may I call you Mitch?" she asked with a provocative tone.

"Absolutely, Noella, he responded immediately looking into her eyes once again but unintentionally holding his gaze. There was something about her that he found very attractive.

"So, Mitch," she paused, "I know you were once a caretaker at Carlton School." She looked him deep in the eyes and noticed he was not surprised by her statement.

He smiled a nervous smile as he stalled for time. "Yes, I was there for just a few brief weeks. I wasn't really happy there and didn't feel it was a healthy place." He looked nervous as Noella explored his facial expressions even further. "How do you know that, by the way?"

"I just do." She said quite matter-of-factly. Noella flipped her hair with her fingers and kept looking at Mitch.

"I also know that you saw something that was … well let's say… a reason why you asked to be transferred out of Carlton." Noella continued to stare at Mitch with a seductive gaze which started to make him feel a bit flustered.

"What do you think I saw?" Mitch asked with a smile and an innocent tone of voice. He knew she must have spoken to someone either in his department or someone closely connected with the school. They looked at each other, her with suspicion and he with a guilty look on his face.

"The asbestos report," she quietly said, almost in a whisper as she continued to play with her long flowing hair. He watched as her fingers twirled the beautiful blonde locks and he almost became entranced by the movement of her fingers. Suddenly he found himself lost in a fantasy with her on a remote beach and …

"Mr. Mason?" Noella suddenly asked as she noticed the glazed look that had come over Mitch's eyes.

Mitch realized he was daydreaming, shook his head a bit and came back to the business at hand. "Sorry Noella," he began, "I was just thinking back to … previously good times. I know it's hard to believe but I did enjoy my work. I'm happy to be here now though!"

"I would hope so," said Noella with a somewhat impatient tone. "Now I would like to see the report we started talking about, Mitch," she added, this time with a seductive and sultry voice. She was hoping to use her charm as she could see that Mitch was somewhat taken with her. "I need it badly … Mitch," she added in a sexy voice.

He was certainly taken by her stunning looks. He wasn't sure how much he should share but he was captivated by this amazingly intelligent and beautiful woman. "Well, Noella," he began with hesitation, "It's not easy for me to share this with you, but I believe I must do so in good conscience since you've been so persuasive … and it is obvious you already know something." Mitch looked nervous and even though he tried to break eye contact with Noella, he couldn't bring himself to do that.

"Your secrets are safe with me," said Noella, again with seductive inflection in her voice. "What happens in your office … stays in your office, Mitch … I just want you to know that…" She gazed at him for a long time until he finally broke eye contact with her. Mitch could see she was trying to use suggestive language as if to suggest a possible intimate encounter. He quickly switched his tone to a formal one.

"Ms. … De Haviland …" he began.

"Please. I told you to call me Noella," she reminded him abruptly.

"Noella … I need you to know this is something we don't take lightly here at the board offices." Mitch started to explain.

"Even though our documents are public record, there are certain things that we don't openly share unless we're forced to by law. What you're asking to see may impact the future of many families and indeed an entire community. Do you still want me to share the information?" Mitch looked at her again and felt an excitement he hadn't felt in a long time.

"Are you married, Mitch?" Noella asked, already knowing the answer. She had done her research on him, as she did with the many people, she did business with.

"Recently divorced actually," Mitch responded with some hesitation. He began to return her gaze more intently at this moment, wondering how she would react and what she might say next.

"Well Mitch … if you've been married, as I have … 3 times actually… you'll know that we can't always get what we want, but there are ways to get what we need when push comes to shove. Now I'm not implying a threat by any means. All I'm saying is that our past sometimes has a way of following us in directions we ... don't always expect."

Noella was studying him intently at this point as he appeared to be growing uncomfortable. "I think I know what you mean, Noella," Mitch began.

"I certainly hope you're not implying anything about my past, because I have nothing to hide." He was now becoming a little annoyed but hoped it wasn't obvious.

"Oh Mitch, ... Mitch ... Mitch. We *all* have something to hide from our past. Skeletons in the closet so to speak. I guess the question is how strongly we feel about ... keeping things private." Noella knew she was getting to him.

Mitch got to his feet and walked around the other side of his desk where Noella was seated. While not getting in her space, he sat down onto the edge of his desk and was silent as he looked at her. Again, he found himself drawn to her, not only in a physical way but there was something about her demeanor ... the power she seemed to exude that both mesmerized and scared him.

While he wondered what she knew, and wasn't impressed that she may have investigated him in some way, his curiosity was so overpowering that he had to know whatever she had on him.

"Ok," he finally said looking down at her and deeply into her eyes. "I'll play along. What deep dark secrets do you know about me?" His tone was serious yet alluring and Noella also found herself once again drawn to the mystery that was Mitch Mason.

Noella flipped her hair and sat up higher in her chair, almost looking like she was ready to stand, but leaning forward on her seat, her cleavage exposed. "I think you already know, Mitch." she suggested in a sultry voice.

The two of them gazed at each other intently, as if waiting for one another to crack. It was not an aggressive look from either one but more of a deep connection and curiosity.

"You've been teasing me this far," stated Mitch, "What's a little bit more?"

He was firing back the sultry voice as well as the looks that he knew would entice her. "Do you really think I'm worried?" he asked Noella who had not broken eye contact with him.

"Well Mr. Mason, you certainly are an intriguing man," Noella began. "I can see how you might have been a very attractive option for your ex-wife and … others who came into your life."

"But I know about some of your escapades at Carlton School, and at other schools for that matter, because you see ... Mitch… I have a lot of friends out there … friends with, shall we say "influence" and not only influence with the Board, but also with local and provincial authorities."

Mitch looked deeply into her eyes, understanding what she was saying. He knew there were secrets. For him, it was how far she was willing to expose them. But somehow, he needed to find out.

The next evening, Lianna decided to take some time with her girls and make dinner. It was Friday night and one of their favorite nights of the weekend. She knew their favorite foods and took extra time to prepare a great meal of prime rib beef with baked potatoes, corn and broccoli with cheese sauce. They also loved fresh bread and so she used the bread maker to make an outstanding loaf. The smell permeated every corner of the house and it was amazing!

The girls came home late after school as they both had volleyball practice. Dallas made the junior team and Diane played for the seniors. They were excellent athletes, as their mother had once been, and were following in her footsteps when it came to school sports teams. Diane also played community basketball as well as soccer and Dallas played slow pitch baseball.

It was now 6:30 P.M. and Lianna was getting worried. It was dark outside and the girls had a 20-minute walk home after practice. Suddenly Lianna heard the door open and a sigh of relief came over her.

"Hi girls!" Lianna cheerfully said. "What did you smell when you walked in?"

"The smell of STRESS!" exclaimed Diane who was clearly frustrated about something.

"Why? Who's stressed?" Lianna replied with a slight chuckle. "I'm actually pretty good. And...," Lianna went on ... "I've made our favorite dinner tonight! Can you guess what's cooking in the oven?"

"What's left of our lives maybe..." Diane said sarcastically as she threw her backpack on the couch. Lianna was starting to get concerned and so she changed her tone to show more empathy for her daughter.

"What's wrong dear?" Lianna replied sympathetically. "Was your day that bad?" She waited for a response and then after a moment of silence, she decided to go over to Diane and give her a hug. Tears began to flow from her daughter's eyes and before speaking, Lianna decided to give it a few seconds. "Do you want to talk about it, Diane?" she asked in a loving voice.

"What's the use Mom," Diane replied. "He's never coming back! I just keep on hoping but the reality is, you're not getting back together with Dad." She began to sob and Lianna tried harder to console her.

Meanwhile, Diane's sister Dallas plopped herself down in front of the TV but was listening in the background.

She decided to add her two cents worth. "Well, if Mom didn't keep ignoring him and run out every time he tried to express his concerns, then maybe he'd still be here!" Dallas stated in a sarcastic tone of voice.

She felt that she was her father's favorite and she defended him in many family disputes. She also felt that Diane was so bitter about their father and didn't give him a fair chance.

"Your father was always trying to avoid conflict and didn't have the balls to speak out!" Lianna responded in frustration. All of a sudden, she realized what she just said and knew that the aftermath wouldn't be good. Dallas almost jumped off the couch and stormed over to her mother.

"Don't talk about him like that!" she screamed as Lianna felt the hurt in her response. "If you weren't working all the time maybe things would be different. *You* were the one who was always avoiding and walking away when he really needed to talk. And *us* too! We all needed to talk and you know I'm right about that, Mom!" Dallas backed away slightly, anticipating what her mom would say or do next.

"That's *NOT* fair Dallas!" Lianna raised her voice. "I was the one keeping things all together when your dad was struggling and you know it. He had his problems too!"

"Maybe, but you didn't try to talk to him enough," responded Dallas. "He felt alone and like he wasn't being heard." There was silence for a moment and then Lianna replied.

"How do you know I never listened to him. I tried so many times but he wouldn't open up and talk." Lianna paused again, waiting for Dallas to come back with something she could work with. Instead, Dallas turned and went back to the couch.

"She's right Mom," interjected Diane. "You were so busy with your stupid principal job and to top it off, sometimes you acted like you owned this place by bossing Dad around, when what you really needed to do was listen."

There was a brief moment of silence and then Dallas spoke. "You weren't fair to him either Diane. You actually were ganging up on him with Mom and the two of you drove him further away from the family!"

Lianna knew that what Dallas was saying to Diane was not wrong, and it made her reflect on the idea. The whole situation was messed up and no one knew just what to do about it. The girls' father had suffered from depression and lost his job a few years back. He was a brilliant computer programmer and after the illness he was really never the same. He began to self-medicate and started drinking more than ever before. This ultimately led to him leaving the house and never returning.

Lianna stayed silent before she spoke once again then offered an olive branch. "Look girls … I know things were difficult in the last few years. We used to have a great family and one that cared very much for each other. I loved your father very much, but things got worse with his depression and…"

"*YOU* drove him to it!" Dallas responded, and then stormed out of the room.

"She's not wrong, Mom," interjected Diane, "you were often too busy and unwilling to have conversations with us when we needed to talk. And especially … with Dad."

Diane started to calm down as she saw the tears well up in her mother's eyes. She knew her mom had regrets about the marriage and was continuing to deal with the aftermath. But she also immersed herself in her work at the school and the girls knew this was Lianna's way of dealing with the separation and divorce. They knew that their mother would just use work as a form of avoidance and they were starting to feel that Lianna was also avoiding them when things got hard.

"I *do* blame him too," Diane said, "Don't get me wrong, and I know he was far from perfect. I just can't help but think there must have been a better way for us all to deal with Dad's problems." Diane paused and continued to look her mom in the eye as Lianna's tears continued to flow. "I'm sorry mom but we have to face the reality that it's just us now. You know we still love Dad and we just wish you would be more willing to talk to him. He is *still* our father and Dallas and I need him in our lives whether you feel that's right or not, or whether it hurts you to see us with him. He is *still* our father."

There was a long silence and suddenly Dallas emerged from her bedroom and entered the kitchen. "So are we gonna eat or what because I'm starving!" Dallas said with hunger in her voice. "Can we just get on with the evening and try to enjoy our favorite meal please?"

"Ok girls," said Lianna as she moved toward the oven. "Dallas is right. Let's eat and maybe we will be less *hangry*. I made this great meal for us and we should enjoy it. You girls deserve it."

The three of them sat at the table exchanging some very trivial and surface level conversation but at least they were civil to each other.

Lianna thought about ways she could make up for lost time but she didn't come up with anything that would ever come close.

Suddenly Diane said, "It's all your fault Dallas. I tried so hard to keep Mom and Dad together, but you did nothing to help mediate between them. At least *I* did!" she added in a hurtful tone of voice.

Dallas said nothing, but dropped her fork on the plate, quietly got up from her seat at the table and walked toward her bedroom again. She was hurt, she was angry, and she felt that her sister had been unfair and was deflecting responsibility away from herself and onto her and her mother.

Lianna wasn't quite sure how she could fix things in the family especially between Diane and her sister. In the meantime, she would have to make sure she cared for them both and showed them the love she still had for them. As a mother, she felt she'd failed and it was time she stepped up and tried to remedy the past, no matter how broken it seemed.

Monday morning came far too fast as Lianna had a terrible sleep

Sunday night. She woke up before her alarm, after tossing and turning, and thinking about Noella and the council meeting.

It was not Lianna's job to keep people happy, but rather do what was best for the students in her school. After all it was a place of education, not a theatre for academy performances. Although Lianna thought Noella created enough drama for everyone.

She started her morning routine, showered and had some coffee, savoring the aroma and enjoying it immensely. This was the only way to start the day and Lianna didn't understand anyone who didn't have coffee first thing. How could anyone function without it?

She drank a little more, then went to her room to get dressed. Her cell phone buzzed and she noticed a text from the Deputy Chief Superintendent who wanted to meet with her later today to talk about Noella. Her stress level rose immediately, as she finished dressing. Then she put on her coat and headed out the door, not sure what the day would bring. What trouble had Noella stirred up now?

Chapter 4

Lianna arrived at the school earlier than usual anticipating that the day would be very hectic. She was used to getting some work done before the teachers came in each day. In fact, Lianna often told her colleagues that she got more done before the staff arrived than she did all day. She started her computer, logged in and opened her email which had 114 messages since yesterday. A principal's work is certainly not easy with all of the communication to read from the system, from parents and from her own staff.

As she read through the messages in front of her, her mind wandered a lot, thinking about a potential meeting with the chief superintendent and she tried to think of a number of responses she might have to a parent complaint. She wasn't sure exactly what Noella might be up to, but she decided it wasn't going to be positive either way. She decided not to worry about it until the moment when she sat with the chief and was asked direct questions about what happened. Had Noella filed an official complaint?

Next, she read the email from the Chief Superintendent and hesitating she opened it. He was requesting a meeting with Lianna and the chair of the Board and himself to discuss the possibility of litigation about the school environment at Carlton School.

Lianna felt confident that she wasn't in any danger of losing her job and that she had behaved professionally with the council and with Noella.

She'd been with the school board for 15 years, starting as a teacher then working her way up as a school administrator, but now she wasn't sure she wanted all these headaches.

The Chief requested a meeting at 3:00 PM at the school and Lianna decided she better oblige so she accepted the meeting request. This made her feel better as she felt that she had the support of her admin and that no matter what Noella threw at her and the school, she knew the board had her back. Or at least she felt they did.

Lianna worked hard to wrap up some of the paper work that hung over her after a busy week last week. The teachers had not yet started to arrive and this was the time when she was able to get lots done without interruption. She felt she'd made a good dent in the pile that was called her "inbox" and was pleased as the school day was soon to begin.

"Good morning, Lianna!" greeted Grade 6 teacher Jason Regere cheerfully as he walked by her office. He popped his head in briefly to ensure she'd seen him arrive early, as some of the staff thought he liked to push the "arrival time envelope".

"Hey Jason," Lianna said with a smile. "You're super early; is everything OK?" Lianna said teasingly. She laughed a bit knowing that she wasn't wrong about this, but also hoped Jason would take it in good fun, which he did.

"Well actually I had a crisis at home this morning," Jason stated, his voice getting quiet with concern."

"Oh really?" Lianna asked, now feeling badly for teasing him about his arrival time. She was genuinely concerned about Jason and his family as they'd been through some difficult times and she hoped they were ok. She knew his wife Samantha and daughter Karina had struggled for a while in their relationships.

"Yes…I'm afraid it's bad this time," Jason paused before continuing, "I'm afraid Samantha has …" again he paused showing intent hesitation.

"Oh, my goodness is it that bad?" asked Lianna with great concern.

"I'm afraid to say," Jason began, "that she's …that she's…oh my God this is painful ...." Lianna now felt terrible and feeling sorry for Jason.

"Go on Jason, you can tell me …," Lianna implored. Jason looked like he had tears in his eyes and Lianna stood up from behind her desk and came around to face him.

All of a sudden, she thought she smelled the scent of onions when she approached him. "She's … finally …" Jason paused again looking very upset and then he spoke, "Exceeded the limit on my Visa card!" he now said in a jesting tone of voice.

He started laughing hysterically and backed away as Lianna motioned to slap him lightly on the arm. Jason was the practical joker on staff and after Lianna remembered this, she was not surprised that he would do this. She then figured out that he created tears using the onion in his pocket, by rubbing his hand and bringing it close to his eyes. She finally smiled and laughed.

"Hey Patricia …," Lianna called out to the school secretary.

"Good morning, Ms. Lianna," Patricia responded as she removed her coat and hung it on the rack in the corner. Patricia had been at Carlton for 10 years or so, and she knew the school and the community inside and out. She was indeed one of the greatest supporters of Lianna and had helped her out of a few tight spots. Patricia called Lianna 'Ms. Lianna', as she came from a very proper British upbringing that taught her respect for her elders as well as her bosses at work. Patricia had arrived from the Philippines about 11 years prior and had worked her way into a school secretary job. The position had been renamed to Administrative Secretary a couple years ago which made the position seem more important.

"Patricia," Lianna began, "I have a critically important meeting with the Chief Superintendent and a couple others at 3:00 P.M. this afternoon. Thought I'd give you a heads up now."

"Very well, Ms. Lianna," Patricia answered, "I'll make sure things are looking just right when they arrive. Do you want me to prepare any refreshments from our staffroom supplies?"

"Let me think about it," Lianna said. "I'm not sure it's an occasion that calls for a little 'sweetening', but I will think carefully about it."

Patricia gave a small head nod and then went to her computer at the front desk where she diligently got to work. Lianna didn't know what she would do without her, as Patricia held the entire office together especially when things got busy and chaotic.

This morning was a typical one, with a couple behavior issues to deal with. Lianna had worked with troubled youth during her university years in a part time job on weekends and she was very familiar with how to deal with behavior problems.

Lianna called a staff meeting at noon for all teachers and support staff who could attend. She explained what had gone on at the council meeting the previous week and how Noella may be creating a bit of a problem in the school. She appeared calm but the staff could tell she was stressed as she announced the upcoming meeting at the school that afternoon.

"We're behind you 100%," said one of the teachers, Caroline Nolan, who'd been at the school for 20 years. "Some of these parents think they can walk all over us … and they're wrong!" she added then went on.

"This parent thinks that because she has money and influence in the community that she can dictate what happens in the school and that is just *NOT* acceptable!" Caroline was passionate about things like this because far too often she'd seen teachers get bullied by power parents in the school. Especially young teachers with less experience.

The meeting soon came to a close and Lianna started heading back to the office ready for the afternoon and to prepare herself for the 3:00 PM meeting. She began to take notes on her computer, trying to recall the exact conversations she had at council and especially those things that Noella had said.

Suddenly, Patricia came to her door and said, "You have a call on line one Ms. Lianna. It's Ms. De Haviland. Would you like me to take a message?" she questioned knowingly.

"No that's fine Patricia. I'll talk to her." Lianna gathered her wits about her and took a couple of deep breaths before picking up the call holding on line 1. Then she picked up the phone and said "Lianna Monahan here. How can I help you?" She immediately felt the stress that was about to ensue in this conversation.

"I have been to the board offices, Lianna," said Noella confidently and condescendingly, "and I'm certain that there's going to be an investigation!" Lianna was silent for a moment and gathered her thoughts before she spoke.

"Oh really, Noella. What about?" Lianna stayed calm and pretended to play innocent as Noella steamed on the other end of the line.

"I met with one high up board official and I have all the information I need to cause you a lot of trouble," Noella stated using a threatening tone. "In fact, Lianna, I would seriously consider getting a lawyer if I were you," Noella added. Lianna again stayed silent for a moment and then spoke.

"What makes you think I'm personally going to need a lawyer?" Lianna asked this time with a little more urgency in her voice.

"You'll find out in time," Noella added, again using a threatening tone. "It's all a matter of time before you won't be in charge of this school…or any school for that matter!"

"I beg to differ, Noella, and as much as I'd love to chat, I need to get on with the business of making sure your children, and all children in this school are safe!" Lianna responded and this time in a more forceful voice. "Have a good day, Noella!" And with that, she hung up the phone.

Noella held on the line and couldn't believe she'd been treated the way she was. She was bound and determined to get her revenge and to see Lianna removed from the principal's position at Carlton School… even if it killed her.

Chapter 5

At 2:55 PM the Chief and deputy superintendents walked through the front door and Lianna was there to greet them in the office.

"Chief Croskenheimer," Lianna said enthusiastically. "Welcome to Carlton School! So good to have you come out, although I wish the circumstances were better."

"Nice to meet you, Lianna. This is Deputy superintendent Richard Hammond, and please … call me Brad," the chief went on. "I'm expecting the chair of the public school board to be here as well. I thought it was important for him to be in the loop with what's going on."

"I totally agree, Brad," said Lianna sounding nervous. "I think the more we're all on the same page the better. Consistent information is going to be critical."

"I couldn't have said it better myself, Lianna," said the chief. We must present a united front if we're going to see a good resolution to this problem."

Lianna felt better that Brad was agreeing with her, and not laying blame on her for Noella's behavior. She knew however that if push came to shove, he would have to do what was necessary to protect the system and that the "Board of trustees", the elected officials, were actually Brad's bosses.

Board chair Chas Upperton arrived momentarily and they all greeted each other before going into the conference room. Chas was a tall man and very well spoken. He was formal, yet friendly and welcoming, and he knew how to connect with people. As an elected official however, he was very careful when it came to situations that could become political for him, so reports of mismanagement or dangerous environments didn't sit well with him.

"So, Brad," Chas began, "what sordid affairs have brought us to this meeting today?' He chuckled immediately trying to keep the conversation on the light side. He looked across the table then made eye contact with Lianna and her Assistant Principal, Michael Kamaguchi, who was feeling unsure of his role at the meeting. He and Lianna had talked but not very much since he heard the chief was coming and he felt a bit unprepared.

"Well Chas, we do have a bit of a dilemma and we were hoping you might help us out with this one." Brad paused for a moment before continuing. "

"A parent of 3 children here at the school has received some information that implicates us in a potential asbestos problem she discovered from old documentation. She requested a copy of a report and states that it is a matter of student safety and security and therefore the documents are open to public record. In other words, she's saying that the reports are not the "private" or intellectual property of the board, but rather open to public scrutiny and accessible according to freedom of information legislation. Unfortunately, I have to agree with her."

Chas was silent for a moment and appeared to be deep in thought. As an elected official, it was his duty to protect the public interest, and yet this matter had the potential to be highly controversial and damaging to the board's reputation. "I'm feeling that there may be no choice but to allow her access here, so we need to plan a strategy to respond to a couple of scenarios."

Brad looked worried and was quiet. He looked at Lianna, who also had a very concerned look on her face and he could tell that her stress level was rising. "I want you to know Lianna, this isn't on you ... the reports are not your fault. As a principal, it's only your responsibility to provide a safe and caring learning environment for your students and to bring any matters of potential risk to our attention ... *if* you know they exist.

You had no way to know about the reports from years ago, as they're more a matter of record keeping in the Facilities department. It isn't their responsibility to provide copies to the school. As you know, many of our old schools have materials that contain asbestos, and it's our responsibility to acknowledge its presence and to ensure the asbestos is remediated and not air born in any way."

"I have to agree with Brad, said Chas. "It's not on you to know about the containment or to fix the problem. It's up to us to keep the school safe." He hoped to reassure Lianna of her innocence. "The caretakers do have access, but they only need access to the reports if they need to make an alteration to the structure, which they are not really allowed to do."

"That's true," added Brad, "It falls more on the caretaker than on you."

"Where would Noella get her information from?" Lianna asked in a puzzled tone of voice. "Did she get it from a former employee or someone who had first-hand knowledge of the building? It had to come from someone like that." Lianna's voice showed her frustration.

"I'm sure it will all work itself out in the end," Michael said, trying to reassure his principal. Michael had a way of staying calm when Lianna needed it most.

"I know, Michael, but I am *so* angry with her. Just because she didn't get her way at council, she's taken it upon herself to cause trouble for us. She has money, power and influence in this community and this will not be good for the future of this school."

"So, as I said," Brad began, "We will need a response for parents if Noella makes this public, but I think we should wait to see exactly where she takes this next."

"I agree, Brad," said Chas as he looked intently at the Chief.

"Have you ever faced something like this before?"

"Years ago, we had a school," began Brad, "that had an exterior wall that was deemed to be potentially unstable. It was in an affluent community, with supportive parents and they had a lot of money, and influence when it came to school decision making." Brad went on to describe how the parents worked together with the school and the Board of trustees to come up with a workable solution. There were also certain parents who donated money to the cause and overall, it turned into a positive experience from a public relations perspective for all involved.

"That's great, Brad." Chas began. "But how do you propose we turn this one around into something that works out well for the school and for the community?" He paused for a moment.

"Just because there is asbestos in the building, doesn't mean we have to go through the complete abatement process. We can't set a precedent for all of our old schools that are in the same situation. We just don't have the resources or the money to do that."

"I realize that, Chas," Brad responded "and that is why this situation is quite different. Here we have a parent who is hell bent to cause trouble rather than work with us. Maybe we need to appeal to her parental side and engage her as a part of the solution."

"Or we need to appeal to her ego and her selfish side and make her a hero for the community," Chas responded.

"What do you mean?" asked Lianna who was confused by Chas' statement.

She really wasn't sure how Noella could ever be considered a hero in the eyes of the community if she was exposing potential danger or harm to their kids. Was Chas trying to play politics with this situation and gain Noella's favor as a person with lots of money?

"What I mean, Lianna," Chas began, "is that maybe we need to make *her* the hero and the person who comes up with the solution for the school." He looked at Lianna intently.

"People like her seem to thrive on recognition and power. If the community sees her as the one that *rescues* the school … she will have that. Don't you think? We use her to help *solve* the problem instead of *being* the problem."

Lianna thought about what Chas said very carefully before speaking. "People like Noella tend to develop very harsh and vindictive mindsets when people cross them. Their egos can't deal with challenges that require them to compromise or engage in win-win situations. I'm fairly new to the principal's role, but I do recognize the narcissistic type of person we're dealing with here. With all due respect to you and your idea, I don't think she'll buy it. She is a narcissist, through and through, and I stand by my judgement of her personality and character." Lianna was assertive in addressing Brad and Chas and she continued eye contact with both.

"You make a convincing argument, Lianna," said Brad, carefully contemplating what she just said. "But if we don't at least try to work with her, we'll be doomed to accept her terms which at this point may not be very positive. If I am right about her."

"She's after my job, Brad. She wants to see me dismissed. The School Act says that I am responsible for my school and if push comes to shove in a court of law, she could get her wish. She openly admitted this to me on the phone earlier today so I am not optimistic about her ability to compromise. She's out for blood!"

"All things considered," said Brad, "You are keeping a stiff upper lip about this and we admire that. Let's see where she goes next, but my vote is to take the position Chas has proposed and try to make her the hero." Brad looked at each person around the table and tried to assess where their heads were at on this.

"Michael, what do you think?" asked Chas, showing respect for everyone's opinions in the room.

"Well, Lianna … you know I try to support you in every way and have the greatest respect for our working relationship." Michael paused before he continued. "In this case however, I tend to agree with Chas' opinion that her ego could be her point of weakness and that we could use it to our advantage."

"Fair enough, Michael." Lianna responded. "Maybe we can appeal to her narcissism and find a way to work around this. I see your point Chas, and I guess I'm willing to try anything to save my reputation and my job." Lianna shifted in her seat and then looked at her watch. "I must excuse myself gentlemen. I need to be at the doors when the bell rings. I always say goodbye to my students as they leave the school."

"That's admirable, Lianna," said Brad, "and this is why you're one of my favorite principals in the system."

"Thank you, Brad," said Lianna humbly and she headed for the conference room door. Lianna made her way to the main door where students were exiting the building.

She stood there waving goodbye and wishing them a good evening at home. This is what she enjoyed most about being a principal… the contact with her students and showing how much she cared about them.

Lianna left the school around 6:00 P.M. after making some calls to parents and meeting with some of her staff. She looked at her calendar in Outlook and realized she had a dinner date scheduled with a principal colleague at 6:30 PM. She panicked a little as she quickly drove home and, on the way, she called Todd to let him know she was running behind schedule.

"I'm so sorry, Todd," she apologized. "I should be there by 6:45 or so."

"No problem," he responded. "I won't give up the reservation. They were going to go to Chez Gaston, a very popular French restaurant in the inner city. Todd invited her to dinner a couple weeks ago and because of their busy lives at home and work, they had to reschedule.

Todd was a single parent of two boys and so he understood the pressures Lianna was under. He was Principal of a large middle school in the suburbs, and had been a school administrator for many years. Lianna respected his opinions and often called him for advice.

She arrived at the restaurant at 6:40 PM, a little earlier than she expected. Todd was seated at a very quiet table that was somewhat removed from others and in a dimly lit corner. There were two candles burning, and immediately she could see a bottle of white wine chilling in the center of the table as well. Her expectations were not high for the evening and she was pleasantly surprised.

He stood up as the Maître D brought Lianna to the table, and pulled out her chair just before she sat down. Her stress level dropped immediately, and she began to feel more relaxed after a long hard day. What would the evening bring? It was only a matter of time before she found out.

Chapter 6

"I'm so glad you could finally make it!" Todd said enthusiastically as she sat down. "I was wondering if you were going to feel like going to dinner given what you've been going through."

"It's actually a very good thing that I'm taking a break from the stress of the job," Lianna replied, "I'm in need of some relief!" Lianna was dead serious but she knew that it would always be in the back of her mind. She was doing her best to compartmentalize and block out thoughts of Noella.

Todd was a perfect gentleman and seemed to recognize Lianna's need to unwind without "shop" talk. He avoided conversation about their schools - including his own – and if she tried to bring up work, he subtly tried to change the subject. He had so much respect for her and he wanted her to know this unequivocally. She didn't yet know it but he actually had strong romantic feelings for her for a long time now but he needed to take his time and first make sure she was comfortable dating a colleague.

They ordered dinner, which consisted of some fine foods, starting with a French Onion Soup, a Chicken and Mushroom Fricassee, Moules Marinieres, followed by dessert of Floating Islands with Dark Chocolate Crème. It was a divine meal they both thoroughly enjoyed.

As dinner went on, they enjoyed each other's company immensely. Their eye contact increased and the conversation was becoming more intimate. While they waited for a desert to come, Todd decided to take a chance.

"So Lianna …there's something I need to ask you …," Todd began, "and I don't want to stress you out or anything, but I need to know …"

"Go on…" Lianna replied enthusiastically. "What do you need to know?"

Todd looked nervous as he didn't want to put any pressure on Lianna, but he couldn't help but feel hesitant. "I know you've been in a long-term relationship with your ex, and I know you've been apart for a few years … but I can't help but wonder if you're over him, and ready to date a colleague." Todd looked into her eyes as if to try to see the truth about what she was about to say.

"I'm totally over my ex!" Lianna said emphatically as she took a sip of her wine. She wanted to make sure he understood this and she looked deep into his eyes so he could tell she was sincere. "I need *you* to know I'm ready to pursue other relationships now, and I wouldn't lead you on, Todd." Lianna gave him a convincing look so he would believe her.

"Well, that's great to hear, Lianna. You know I've admired you since I first met you. Even before you were a principal." Todd went on, "I also know how hard it must have been raising those two lovely girls on your own, but also having to deal with a difficult ex-husband. I raised my boys but that was after my wife passed away so at least I didn't have to deal with an ex like you do."

Lianna was empathetic and realized how hard Todd's loss must have been. She did have to deal with a difficult ex as he'd said, but that was completely different. "I'm so sorry about your wife," Lianna explained sympathetically. "Nothing can replace a parent in situations like that and I do feel for your boys. At least my girls can see their dad once in a while."

"No need to be sorry," Todd said trying to be strong as he remembered his former wife and the mother of his children. "She was very sick and once the cancer reached a certain point, there was no quality of life anymore." He was quiet for a moment, so Lianna did the same, allowing him to reflect.

After a minute or so of silence, Lianna spoke. "So, Todd … I really do want you to know that I love spending this time with you. We've been friends for a long time and I never want that to change. But I also feel that maybe we have more to explore with each other."

Lianna wondered whether she'd crossed a line with this comment, but suddenly saw happiness return to Todd's face, as it was when she arrived. This was a relief, as she didn't want the evening to turn into a sad time for either of them.

"I'm so glad you feel that way, Lianna. I've always wondered about you and me as a couple." Todd paused, choosing his next words carefully. He didn't want to scare her off either, and he now realized maybe they felt the same way about pursuing a relationship.

Todd insisted on paying the bill and after dinner they went for a walk by the river. The sun was just starting to set and the sky was a rainbow of colour. Lianna was so happy to be with a man who was so supportive at this difficult time in her career. But she always put up a very strong front and didn't want people to see her vulnerabilities.

As a principal, weakness was never something she believed she should show … even to her own family. The girls always looked up to her as a very stable mother who didn't get easily flustered or upset. She was a calm and rational mom that thought through things very carefully and made decisions based on logic rather than impulsive reactions.

They strolled on the picturesque path above the river and came to an elevated area where they could clearly see the sun setting on the horizon.

Both Todd and Lianna loved all the breathtaking colours and the billowy clouds scattered across the multicolored sky.

"It's absolutely breathtaking, isn't it?" Lianna said to Todd.

She looked at him with a look of admiration and respect as he turned to meet her gaze with his own.

"Beautiful!" he responded. He was looking at her and she sensed that he was no longer talking about the sunset anymore. They gazed deeply into each other's eyes and for a moment, all their worries and concerns, all the stress they experienced today had gone from their minds and bodies.

This ... was what matters in the end – a relationship where two people care for each other.

Todd took a step closer to Lianna, reached for her hand which she happily moved toward his. Her body moved naturally closer to him as well, and for a moment it was like their hearts were one and the same. Todd brought his head closer, but ever so slowly to hers. She closed her eyes as if to say, *yes please kiss me*. At that very moment, a cyclist came by on the path they stood beside and rang his bell to warn them of his approach. They both pulled away and suddenly started laughing, both wondering if a kiss was meant to be. The mood quickly changed from one of romance to humor.

They continued to walk along the river and the daylight seemed to be disappearing more rapidly than they realized. Lianna's place was not far from where they were and they didn't want the night to end. They headed back to the restaurant to get their vehicles.

"Are your girls at home this week?" Todd asked as they arrived back at their cars. Todd was hesitant to ask the question, but he figured he had nothing to lose.

"As a matter of fact," Lianna began, "they are with their dad right now. As you know, they alternate weeks with me and my ex."

Lianna knew what Todd was asking, and she didn't mind. Actually, she became hopeful the evening wouldn't end here. "Would you be interested …" she began, "in coming to my place for a nightcap?" Lianna smiled as she said the words and Todd reciprocated.

"Well …" Todd decided to tease her a little, "that depends …". He looked more intently into her eyes.

"What would it depend on?" Lianna queried, very curious to hear what he had to say.

"How tasty the nightcap is," Todd answered suggestively.

"Ohhhhh, it could be *very* tasty." Lianna teased him with her seductive tone.

"I guess I'll have to take my chances," Todd said decisively. He continued to gaze into her eyes, and he moved in closer wanting to kiss her.

This time, there was no cyclist to interrupt and the two of them embraced in a passionate kiss that sent shivers through both of them. They held the kiss for at least a minute, both not wanting to release. Finally, a person from the restaurant came walking by and they decided to exercise restraint as the woman passed.

"Nice night for that sort of thing," the woman boldly said to Todd and Lianna. They chuckled and she passed by as if nothing had happened. Todd and Lianna both laughed.

"I guess we *better* get a room as some people used to say," Todd added to ease some of the embarrassment. Lianna laughed once again and then started to take out her car keys.

"You know how to get to my place?" she asked him.

"Oh yes," he said, "how could I forget?" Todd had been to visit her on a number of occasions, including Lianna's 35th birthday party that her girls surprised her with. Todd helped them organize it after they called asking him to invite some of her friends.

"We'll see you there then. I'll meet you at my entrance," she said seductively. Lianna was more certain of her attraction to Todd after the amazing kiss. Not only was he healthy and in good shape, he was also super intelligent with a great reputation and a great career, hoping to work in the district office as a superintendent someday.

Lianna started her car and drove off and Todd was not far behind her. He parked his car across the street from her building. Lianna emerged from the underground carpark moments later, and Todd began to walk toward her.

"This is such an amazing building," Todd said, admiring the modern features. "Ever have thoughts of wanting to move to a house though? You know, with a back yard and maybe a large patio with a BBQ and all?"

Lianna looked at him and said, "Why isn't my balcony barbeque enough? *and* …I don't have to cut grass or shovel snow!" she added, almost flaunting her good fortune.

"You have a good point there," Todd laughed. Lianna loved to hear his laugh, as it made her feel secure in many ways. Her father had been a good man who always tried to find humor or laughter in any situation … good or bad.

Lianna entered the security code to the front door, then another code to enter the interior door. Todd felt he was entering a very secure building and he was happy for this.

"So … maximum security," Todd began, "Any chance of parole after a few years?" Together they both laughed and continued on inside where Lianna had to enter yet another code at the elevator. They looked at each other knowingly and laughed again.

"Good evening, Ms. Monahan," said the concierge, whose name was Alfred. He was a very nice man and excellent at his job. Lianna knew he had her best interest at heart, and she greatly appreciated that. He reminded her of her late father who had looked out for her even after she moved out of his house.

"Hey Alfred … how are you tonight?" she asked him with genuine interest.

"Doing just fine," he said, "but kind of missing talking to your lovely girls this week." Alfred loved to see Diane and Dallas every day as they left for school or when they arrived home.

They were like his 'adopted daughters', and he cared about them both. Alfred had never married nor had any kids and Lianna knew that her girls were special to him as he greeted them every day.

"You remember my good friend Todd."

"Oh yes," Alfred responded. "I certainly do. Good to see you again, Sir."

"Likewise, Alfred," Todd responded. "I just love your building here!" said Todd with a complimentary voice.

"It's my favorite place of all time. But it's the *people* that make it that way," said Alfred in a sentimental voice as he looked with admiration at Lianna. "Well … have a good night together," he said. Lianna and Todd both looked at each other and smiled. They both knew what Alfred's words could imply. But neither of them seemed to care.

Chapter 7

Lianna opened the door to her place, and invited Todd inside. He was a little nervous as he'd never been here alone with her before. There were always people around to be a "buffer" between them but now it was just the two of them.

"Do you want the big *tour*?" Lianna asked him as he took off his shoes and glanced around the living room. She could tell that Todd was a bit nervous, and there was still a bit of tension … some apprehensiveness on his part that she thought made him a little quieter than usual. "Are you ok?" she asked noticing his silence.

"I'm ok," he replied, "Remember this isn't my first time here at your place." He smiled at her and this somewhat eased her concern.

"Well, I just want you to feel at home here, no matter what," Lianna added. "The girls won't be coming home for three more days, and I'm also sure they like you a lot."

"Thanks, Lianna," said Todd as he went toward her 34th story window. He loved looking out at the mountains from here. "I just love the view from up here."

Lianna could feel that Todd was starting to feel more relaxed, and she decided to offer him a drink. "How about that nightcap I mentioned earlier?" she asked him with a sultry tone in her voice.

"That's a great idea," Todd said. "What do you propose?"

Lianna gazed at Todd for a moment and then responded.

"Well ..." she began, "I have several choices actually.

I have a great peanut butter whiskey, I have Irish Mist, Grand Marnier, cognac or wine if you'd prefer." Lianna loved peanut butter whiskey and hoped he would pick that.

"You had me at peanut butter," Todd said, almost reading her mind. "Who could resist a good PBW?

"An excellent choice!" Lianna said with enthusiasm. "Just give me a minute. Would you like yours neat or on ice?"

"Two ice cubes would be great," Todd said decisively. Lianna turned and went to the pantry where she kept a variety of spirits, including the peanut butter whiskey.

Todd continued to enjoy the view of the mountains, looking at the remaining silhouettes across the horizon as darkness descended on the city. He was hopeful that Lianna was comfortable with him here in her place and he'd do anything to help her feel that way.

Lianna called from the kitchen to Todd. "Can you still see the mountains Todd, or is it too dark now?" she asked.

"If you hurry, we'll catch the tail end of the sunset," Todd explained with urgency. Shortly after that Lianna appeared with their drinks in two beautiful crystal rock glasses. She handed one to Todd.

"I'd like to propose a toast ...," she said. "Here's to a great evening together!" and she raised her glass toward Todd who reciprocated immediately. They looked at each other and without breaking eye contact, took a small sip of their drinks. Neither of them wanted to be the first to look away. After a moment, they both turned to look out at the mountain silhouettes and continued to savor their drinks. Neither spoke for a minute or so, as they were just enjoying the view as the city lights slowly took over the foreground.

"I am so happy you're here tonight, Todd." Lianna said in a calm and quiet voice. She moved closer to him, and she began to feel butterflies as they stood side by side. She wondered if Todd was feeling the same thing, then suddenly, he turned toward her and without a word, he kissed her cheek. She turned to face Todd with a gentle smile that melted his heart.

"I want you to know that I'm crazy about you Lianna… always have been," Todd said with a loving tone of voice. "We've known each other for years now and I've always valued your friendship. You are smart and funny, so good with kids and with your staff, not to mention … a great kisser!" They both chuckled and Lianna then moved closer expecting a more intimate exchange. Todd placed his hands on either side of her face and pulled her closer as their lips met in the most passionate kiss Lianna had ever felt. She sighed softly as their mouths opened wider to exchange an even more intimate moment.

They held this for what seemed like some time, then Todd wrapped his arms around Lianna, and pulled her body tight against his. The passion was growing, as they shared each other's energy.

There was a moment where they separated, then Lianna, seeing the timing was right, said to Todd, "Do you want me?".

"Very much so!" Todd responded, now yearning deeply for her. They were both a little scared but they knew they had to submit to each other at the same time if things were to progress. Lianna reached for the buttons on Todd's shirt, and starting at the top very slowly made her way down, unbuttoning them one by one.

"Are you sure?" she said as she began to kiss him on the neck slowly. Todd let out a soft moan as she started to slide the shirt from his shoulders to reveal his very well-toned body.

"More than ever!" Todd replied as he helped her remove his shirt. Reaching out for her blouse, he slowly began to unbutton it as he kissed her neck gently, nibbling lightly on her skin as he moved his mouth down toward her chest. He reached around to unhook her bra, which fell to the floor as they both stood topless facing each other. He continued to kiss her neck, then made his way downward to taste her breasts, first one then the other, as his tongue danced in circles around her perfect nipples.

She threw her head back, her hair waving back and forth between her shoulder blades as she immersed herself in the pleasure of Todd's touch. Soon she couldn't take it anymore and she reached for the button on his pants. Todd knew what was going to happen next.

"Are you sure?" he asked, as he felt the zipper slowly being pulled down. She was kissing him but stopped and gazed into his eyes. Lianna wanted him so badly, but she didn't want him to think she was easy. She also needed him to know that if they did this, it meant they were now in a serious relationship.

"Only if you are," she responded. "Things are going to change now Todd," she said in a whisper.

"I know," he responded, "I'm a little afraid, but I know that I'm crazy about you Lianna." With this, she pulled down his pants, pushed him onto the couch then removed them.

He lay there in his boxers now and she could see his manhood full of enthusiasm in the front. It had been so long since she had any encounter like this with a man and she was more than ready.

Lianna moaned softly as she lowered her face above the front of his boxers. She was on her knees beside the couch and ever so slowly reached into the bottom of his boxers. As soon as she found his now pulsing member, he moaned and this drove her even more crazy.

He could feel her hot breath against his boxers as she placed her teeth on the waistband. She grabbed on and pulled them to his ankles, all the time keeping eye contact with him as she wanted his manhood desperately, and he knew it. But Todd wanted her to have some control. It would have been so easy to let her please him in that moment but he wanted to hold back.

"Lianna … I …" Todd began, "I want you desperately, but I also want to make sure I please you."

"Oh, you certainly are," Lianna responded. "More than you'll know." She moved closer to his manhood. He tried to raise his chest as if to get up but she gently forced him onto his back again. He decided not to resist, but he would only let her go so far. She began to please him as only a woman knows how. His hard body lay there but he actively engaged in what she was doing. He felt his passion rising quickly so he stopped her just before his release.

"Your turn Lianna…," he said in a very sultry tone of voice. He stood up and reached for the top of her skirt, where he found the clasp. It fell to the floor to reveal her sexy G-string which barely covered her womanhood. Todd let out a low-pitched moan as she stood before him in all her glory. Naked. Exposed. Vulnerable. She wanted him so badly.

He got down on his knees in front of her, and without saying a word, he slowly moved his lips closer and closer to the G-string.

He reached around and grabbed her buttocks with each hand, pulling her even closer. She could feel his hot breath, rapid and strong through the material.

"Taste me," she said in a sexy whisper. He pulled the triangular front aside to reveal what was the most beautiful womanly arrangement he'd ever seen. He could see the faint glistening of her excitement, oozing slowly from within her perfect petals.

Suddenly, she grasped the back of his head and pulled it directly onto her. Todd grabbed her buttocks more firmly as he tasted her forbidden fruit. She ground herself against his mouth, moaning loudly as his lips and tongue brought her to ultimate pleasure. In moments, she had reached the peak of excitement and didn't hold back. She screamed in ecstasy as wave after wave of gratification pulsed through her entire body.

Todd was now highly aroused and he removed her G-string, picked her up, and took her to the bedroom. "Yes Todd … I need you!" Lianna said out loud giving him permission as he set her lovingly down on the bed.

She drew her legs up high while Todd stood on the floor at the edge of the bed. He knew she was ready and full of desire. He stood over her gazing deep into her eyes and brought his manhood closer to her. She moved her hips forward to receive him and for a moment, he rested it against her.

"Please Todd," Lianna pleaded. He finally succumbed to her beckoning, and with one passionate thrust, he crossed the threshold of her desire.

With every motion, one after another, Lianna met his with her own, wanting him to know he was the only one for her. In moments, and without notice, his manhood exploded with wild abandon. Pulse after pulse of his desire shot deeply into her and he cried out in ecstasy as she continued to thrust back even after his waves had subsided.

When he was finally devoid of all remaining energy, she grasped his hand and pulled him onto the bed beside her. Together they lay, she on his chest, and his arms around her. "Wasn't that the best night cap you've ever had?" Lianna asked him.

"Nothing will ever compare," he replied as they continued to cuddle and eventually fall asleep. This would go down in history as Lianna's best dinner date ever.

Chapter 8

Lianna woke up to a delicious smell coming from her kitchen as well as the aroma of fresh coffee brewing. She noticed that Todd was out of bed before her and she now knew why. She decided to savor the moment and lay there in bed just a little longer to the sound of Todd cooking breakfast. It was a moment of sheer pleasure, but nothing could come close to what she experienced the night before.

"Hey sunshine," Todd came in the room with a fresh coffee for her. "I thought we should have something to eat before work today, although I wish we could stay in bed all day." Lianna smiled and motioned with her finger for him to come closer. She looked very sexy as she sat on the bed with only a pure white sheet over her, breasts barely covered but shoulders and legs exposed, suggestively positioned for Todd to see. She knew exactly what she was doing.

"Oh my," Todd said as he approached her, wondering what she might do next.

"See anything you like, Todd?" Lianna asked in a very sexy voice.

"I'm certainly taken with your beauty," Todd replied as he placed a hand on her shoulder. She reached for his fingers and interlocked them with hers, hoping he would take the hint.

In the next moment, Lianna let the sheet fall to the bed, leaving her body fully exposed. "Oooops!" she said as she smiled and pulled Todd toward her, reaching to give him a passionate kiss. He sat on the bed and eagerly reached for her, and as they embraced, their passion rose once again. Before long, breakfast was forgotten as they made love with even more intensity than the night before.

****

"That was amazing!" Todd said to Lianna as they got out of bed to go to the kitchen for breakfast. "I never knew just how sexy you could be," he added.

"This morning and our night together are only the beginning of many incredible times, Todd. I intend to immerse us both in some of the most amazing intimate moments," Lianna said with conviction, as they made their way to the kitchen to eat.

"Have a seat, my love," Todd said to her, as he made his way to the oven where some delectable food was being kept warm for them. "There's eggs benedict, maple bacon, sourdough toast, real potato hash browns, fruit, and of course orange juice and coffee… a breakfast certain to start your day right."

Todd was happy to display his culinary skills for his new love, and she was even more pleased to be on the receiving end of this amazing effort…especially before work.

"This is incredible Todd!" Lianna complimented him. "You are a true talent, both in the kitchen … and the bedroom!" she added with a naughty tone of voice.

They both laughed, as Todd served her a plate of food at the kitchen island they enjoyed on several occasions. "Not to spoil the mood at breakfast Lianna," Todd began, "but what do you think you're going to do about Noella, and her latest antics?"

"Well …," Lianna began, "Chas thinks we should try to appeal to her ego and make her a *hero* by letting some of this play out. She would get the credit for bringing it to the awareness of the school community and the board would respond with appropriate action for remediation. But we have to keep it out of the media, I think. The other way might be for me to let council know what

she is up to and take the fun out of it for her."

Todd looked at her and thought for a moment. "I think there's validity in appealing to her ego for sure. Is there any way to do both? To talk to your council before they get the news from her, but also make her think she's exposing it all?"

"Problem is …" Lianna tried to talk and eat at the same time, "Noella has her friend Lindsay Bordeaux on executive, so she'd have to be kept in the loop."

"Unless …" Todd began, "she somehow misses a memo about the exec meeting." He smiled and they both knew what he was suggesting.

"I'll give it some thought Todd, but I think you may be on to something.

They finished breakfast and got ready to head to their respective schools. Taking the elevator down, they were greeted by Alfred before they left the building. "Good to see you two getting along so well." Alfred smiled knowingly, as did Todd and Lianna. "Have a great day, kids!" he added.

"You too Alfred!" Todd and Lianna both said simultaneously and laughed at their perfect timing. They continued toward their cars and as they parted, they embraced in a passionate kiss that lasted for quite some time.

"Call me," said Lianna. "I'll let you know if anything else comes up about Noella."

"Last night was amazing!" Todd said. "A night I will never forget." He turned and headed toward his car.

Lianna headed for the carpark, but as she exited the stairwell, she noticed a man watching her from a distance which made her feel very uneasy. When she drove out of the carpark, the man was no longer there.

****

Lianna arrived at school not long before the students. She organized her thoughts about a plan to call an executive meeting, and how she might do that without letting Lindsay know. She would have to go through council chair Maryanne who of course had her back. That is where she would start.

Lianna greeted Patricia as she passed by the front desk, and headed straight to her office. She closed the door behind her and looked up Maryanne's number and immediately called her.

"Ok Maryanne…I think I have an idea, but I need to ask you as a friend to keep this conversation confidential. Can you do that for me?" Lianna pleaded with Maryanne. Lianna explained the information and accusations Noella was about to bring forward, which didn't surprise Maryanne, and Maryanne listened with a sympathetic ear. She of course held Lianna in the highest regard.

"I'm more than happy to do that for you Lianna, as long as I know you'll defend me with Noella," Maryanne replied. Lianna agreed.

They spoke for a few minutes about calling an executive meeting and Maryanne agreed she would send a memo to executive, but be selective about who she invited. Somehow, Lindsay Bordeaux would not be on the list.

Lianna greeted her students as she always did at the doors, and paid a visit to all the classrooms to say good morning. Todd was always impressed by this, but it was a habit that Lianna learned from some of her best administrators. The staff and students were always happy to say good morning to her as she made her morning "rounds".

The day was otherwise uneventful at the school; however, Maryanne had called the emergency executive meeting of council for 3:15 P.M. Several members gathered including the council secretary and 5 others which included Maryanne and Lianna.

They decided to meet in an empty room away from the office and not in their usual place. "So Lianna ...," Maryanne began, "Can you please fill us in on what is going on with Noella. It seems as though she's discovered some information that could be upsetting to some of us.

"Thank you, Maryanne," Lianna responded. "Noella has obtained information about a potential problem with asbestos in our school. The maintenance department does their due diligence to ensure that a school is safe and that there's no exposed material that could be harmful to students or staff, and they put that information into a report." Lianna paused for a moment.

"What's not commonly known is that because of the age of many schools in our city, there is a great amount of asbestos in old building materials. Now a lot of that is hidden in walls and floors and doesn't present an immediate risk to people. But if it is exposed or disturbed in some way, and it becomes air born there can be risk to people in the building." She paused again and looked at the other executive members.

"I've also been reassured that our school has been tested and inspected to ensure that all asbestos containing materials are not exposed to the open air, and that they meet the current government safety requirements as far as being contained." She hoped this would ease the executives' minds.

"So, Noella has found this report which she says indicates potential hazards, and she plans to expose this information to all of you and the community. She also wants me to be fired, which I believe is a reaction to our last debate about fine arts money," Lianna added.

The executive members were quiet for a moment then the treasurer, Candace Carbone spoke. "Well, Lianna if you tell us that everyone is safe and the board has taken the proper measures to ensure that safety, then we believe you and we'll stand behind you."

"Thank you for your confidence, Candace," Lianna said. "I don't believe she's going to leave this one alone however, which is upsetting. If she can find one piece of evidence to implicate negligence on my part, or the board's, she'll pursue litigation. She told me to get a good lawyer."

"I would have to agree with Candace that our executive will stand behind you, Lianna. Is there anyone opposed to this?" Maryanne asked. She looked around the table and saw unanimous support. "What's our next steps?" Maryanne asked.

"So, the board has agreed that we need to appeal to Noella's ego and let her *think* she's exposing a scandalous report." Lianna began. "We'll let her bring this to the next council meeting and she'll think it's going to be devastating to the school and community. I will have back-up from the Chair, Mr. Upperton, who I will say is there for a regular visit, as he does with all schools throughout the year. He'll downplay the report, as will I, and we'll thank Noella for bringing it to the attention of council and that we'll do an immediate investigation to ensure the safety of all those at the school. She will feel like a hero and hopefully this will appease her."

"I think it's a great idea!" said Millie, "and I think it will satisfy Noella's narcissistic personality needs… Oh, did I just say that out loud?" There was laughter in the room and Lianna felt better already.

"Ok, then I will allow Noella to add the item to the next agenda, as I'm sure she will be requesting an audience. Are we all agreed on this then?" Maryanne asked.

"All in favor? ... Opposed? …Very well then. Seeing no objections, I'd say this is settled," said Maryanne happily as unanimous support was shown.

The meeting adjourned and Lianna went back to her office, only to discover an email from Noella sent that afternoon. As she opened it and started reading, she realized their plan might now be compromised. She would have to call Maryanne to share the news.

Chapter 9

It certainly was a wrench in their plan. Noella had just informed Lianna that she planned to bring lawyers to the meeting and she was sending out a special notice to all parents in the school regarding a potentially hazardous environment, inviting them to the next meeting.

Lianna picked up the phone and called Maryanne so they could plan a response strategy. She knew that if Noella published a flyer to advertise the meeting that the problem would increase tenfold.

"Maryanne?" Lianna said quickly as her call was answered. "Oh, I'm so glad I caught you at home!"

"Hi Lianna, what's going on?" Maryanne asked in a very concerned tone of voice.

"We thought we had a foolproof plan, but I should have known better than to underestimate Noella," Lianna replied.

"Agreed. So, what's up?" Maryanne was curious. "Did Noella threaten you again?"

"Not exactly …" Lianna replied, "but she has ramped up her strategy a little … well actually a lot!" Lianna sound worried and Maryanne followed suit.

"What's going on exactly?" Maryanne queried.

"Noella is now printing custom invitations to send out to all parents asking them to come to the next meeting of council because there's a huge health problem that needs to be addressed." Lianna was emphatic in her words and Maryanne could tell she was worried.

"Has anyone seen the notice yet?" Maryanne asked. "Doesn't she need approval from the office for things like that?"

"She's using a school council email list from last year, but most parents are still on it," Lianna explained. "She's going to reach most of our current population with the mass email. She doesn't really care if it's approved or not. She'll say it's her right as a parent to share the news."

"Not if she's going to scare the crap out of everybody!" Maryanne vocalized emphatically. Maryanne never did agree with Noella's tactics and certainly didn't agree this time. "She's got to be stopped. Is there anything we can do to prevent the email from going out?" Maryanne asked further.

"I think it may be too late. Can you check with someone who's not on council quickly to see if they got the message?' Lianna asked.

"Yes…right away. Hold on …" Maryanne answered quickly, put Lianna on hold and started to call a parent she knew from the school. She came back to Lianna in about one minute with the news. "I'm afraid you are right, Lianna. Noella sent out the message a couple hours ago so we'll have to come up with a plan again."

"Damn it!" Lianna exclaimed in frustration. "She seems to have the upper hand on us for now. Well, that's going to have to change. Let me do some thinking and you do the same, Maryanne. I've got to run, but we'll be in touch soon."

"Absolutely Lianna. Take care my friend," said Maryanne sympathetically.

"You too." said Lianna, appreciating her friend's comment. Lianna really wasn't sure how they should go forward from here. Should she call the chief to get advice? For once in a long time, she was totally unsure what to do.

****

"Call for you on line one Ms. Lianna," announced Patricia over the PA system. Lianna called the office. "Hi Patricia … do you know who the call is from?" asked Lianna, suspicious of whether it was Noella calling with more bad news.

"It's Todd Hackman for you Miss," answered Patricia, knowing that Lianna would be relieved.

"Thank you, Patricia. I'll be there in a moment." Lianna left the classroom quickly, apologizing to the teacher she had been talking with.

She rushed down the hallway toward the office, quickly past the front desk, closed the door then reached for the phone. "Hey Todd," said Lianna happily, but a little out of breath, "hope I didn't keep you waiting too long."

"Not at all, Lianna," Todd replied. "I'm just glad you're available to talk." Todd's voice sounded soothing to Lianna, especially right now when tensions were high with Noella. She told him what Noella was doing with the notice to parents and asked for his advice.

"Well …it's a tough one, Lianna," said Todd. "She certainly has some influence in your community, but I think sometimes it is best to let this kind of parent sink their own ship so to speak. If you feel that she's going to make herself look bad eventually then maybe it's best to sit back a bit and let it happen." Todd was silent for a moment, letting Lianna think about what he was proposing.

I've had parents like this and 9 times out of ten, they'll show their true colors and other people realize that they are really all about themselves and not trying to help anyone else."

This made a lot of sense to Lianna who thought carefully about it. "I think you may be right Todd. It's just hard to sit back and give up control especially with this woman. She gets under my skin for sure."

"And that's exactly what you don't want to let her see," said Todd wisely. "She *wants* to trigger you …set you off course and catch you at your worst. You need to show her who is stronger, smarter and really in control."

"That is excellent advice, Todd." replied Lianna. You're such a wise and intelligent man! Not to mention…*verrrry* sexy!"

"Why thank you!" Todd responded. "Now speaking of getting *under your skin* …When can I get there again? I love the feel of it!" Todd was being very forward but Lianna loved it.

"Maybe this weekend?" she said. "What are you doing Saturday night?" She hoped he would be free because she needed to feel him close to her again. She had been smitten by his charm and his compassion. She wanted him desperately, and there was no denying this now.

"I'm all yours, Lianna. Do you want me to cook you dinner at my place? My boys are going camping for the weekend," Todd explained with enthusiasm. He was hoping her answer would be yes as he couldn't wait to spend more time with her. "I promise you won't be disappointed in my culinary skills," he jested and laughed out loud.

"That sounds absolutely wonderful!" Lianna responded, barely able to contain her excitement. "I promise to eat whatever you put in front of me," she added.

"That sounds … interesting…" said Todd, as Lianna realized her double entendre.

"Well …you know what I mean," chuckled Lianna, with slight embarrassment.

"Great!" Todd answered. "Let's say 5:00 P.M. Saturday at my place then?"

Lianna was over the moon, but she didn't want to show too much enthusiasm. "Sounds good, Todd. Just text me the address, OK?" she said as someone knocked on her office door. They said goodbye and Lianna went to see who was at her door, and she wasn't pleased when she saw who was standing on the other side.

****

Lianna took a moment to compose herself, and wondered where Patricia was. Then she remembered that Patricia had to leave early for a doctor's appointment and no one was covering the front office. She opened the door with hesitation but she knew she had to be strong.

"Noella," Lianna said coolly. "How can I help you today?" Lianna really wasn't ready for a conversation, but as principal it was her job to engage parents as best she could. "I didn't see you in my appointment calendar. Did you set something up with Patricia?"

"That's so cute!" said Noella. "Actually, I just wanted to give you a copy of the notice I sent out to the community via email earlier today. Have you seen it?" Noella asked.

"Not yet …just heard about it," Lianna responded. Noella reached into her leather bag and pulled out a bright pink piece of paper.

"This ought to get their attention," Noella said defiantly. "The brighter the better in my mind."

"I can see why you 'd say that," Lianna said sarcastically. She began reading the notice which started with the words, *Asbestos Scare in Carlton School*. Lianna tried to hide her anger but she didn't think it was working. She looked at Noella and finally asked, "Why are you doing this Noella?"

Noella looked at her for a moment and the two women stared each other down. It was almost as if an old-fashioned duel was about to happen. Neither one broke eye contact until Noella said, "Because … you're not fit to run this school and I intend to prove that!"

"What makes you think that, Noella?" Lianna asked desperately trying to hide her anger once again. Lianna thought about how she would respond to any lame excuse Noella was likely to throw at her.

"It doesn't take a genius to know that you're inexperienced and sadly incompetent. I can see it in you every time you address the council, and I don't want my children to have a weak principal. If you were more assertive that would be one thing but you don't instill confidence in others … especially me!" Noella finished speaking and then waited for a response from Lianna. Lianna was quiet for about 10 seconds, taking control of the situation and finally she decided to speak.

"Ms. De Havilland … I've been an educator for almost twenty years and I know my profession better than many. I've worked with outstanding principals who have taught me a great deal about dealing with children and yes …even parents like you. You are not the first one to try to cross my path and you certainly won't be the last. When it comes to my school and my job, I will defend them both to the bitter end, in spite of any accusations or falsehoods that some people might choose to dream up. If you don't have any solid evidence of my incompetence, then I suggest you refrain from any further slanderous conversation before *you* need a lawyer. Do I make myself clear?" Lianna's heart was racing but she felt a sense of pride. "I think this meeting is over!"

Lianna opened the door and gestured for Noella to leave her office. Noella stood there for a moment with her mouth wide open and then spoke. "You're going to regret your words, *MISS* Monahan!" and then she turned and stormed out of the office.

Lianna knew this wouldn't be the last time Noella would be in her office and in fact, it would be sooner than they both knew.

Chapter 10

Lianna immediately got on the phone to call the chief superintendent's office as she wanted to talk to him before Noella did. While this was all frustrating, she knew it was all part of the "game" that had to play out with Noella. She now had the notice Noella created and she felt better knowing its contents.

While it was difficult to take, she now knew what she was up against as the notice was very clear about the community standing up for their rights and the safety of their children in the school.

"Hello, Brad," Lianna said cheerfully. "Yes, I'm doing well," she answered after a brief pause, "Noella was just in my office as a matter of fact." They conversed for about ten minutes as she described her exchange with Noella. The chief was empathetic and complimented Lianna for standing up for herself and what was right. Lianna also felt better after the chief agreed with what Todd had said about letting Noella *dig her own grave*, so to speak.

"So now I need to deal with the notice," Lianna said. "Should I send my own email to the community?" Lianna knew it was important for her to bring the chief into the loop and he appreciated that.

"Yes, I think it's a good idea, Lianna. Because this is a highly sensitive matter, please send me a copy for preview first. It's not that I don't trust you because I do but that way, I can protect you if things get worse." The chief was sincere and made sure Lianna knew he was on her side.

"I think we need to reassure the community that the notice does not imply immediate risk, and that the Maintenance department has mitigated the dangers in the past by ensuring safe containment of the areas in question."

"Thank you, Brad." Lianna responded. "I sure appreciate all the advice and I will send you a copy of the letter before I send it out to my parents."

They said goodbye and Lianna decided to get right to work on the email but took a walk through the school to check on classrooms first. As she walked, she thought about the way she would word her email to parents, and she was glad for this time to clarify some of her thoughts about the kids and how much she cared for them.

She made her way back to her office with a clear head and ready to begin her message to the community. She began her email with a sentence that showed her appreciation for all the support the parents have given to the school on a daily basis and then began to refer to the notice emailed out by Noella to parents. She assured them that it wasn't a notice authorized by the school and that it contained both false information as well as omitting some truths.

She heard a knock at the door and it was Patricia. "Ms. Lianna, the phone is ringing constantly and everyone wants to know about the pink email sent out by Noella. What should I tell them?"

Patricia seemed overwhelmed and Lianna reassured her that she was taking action to slow down the phone calls.

"Thank you, Patricia. I know this is hard on you and I'm sorry. I'm just about finished an email to parents. For those who call, please tell them that I will be sending an email today explaining what is going on and not to worry. Tell them I didn't authorize the notice they got and they will get accurate information shortly. I'm so sorry, Patricia. You can let some of the calls go to voicemail if you'd like. I know you have so much other work to get done."

"It's ok, Ms. Lianna. I'm here for you and will do my best," Patricia replied and she went back to answering the phones.

"Thanks so much, Patricia," Lianna called after her, "I don't know what I'd do without you!"

Lianna finished up the email and sent it to Brad for approval. In a few minutes, she had the go-ahead from the Chief, so she then sent it to all parents on the school's contact list. She hoped that her words would ease the minds of the parents and after all, her school had passed both provincial and municipal safety standard inspections for asbestos. She was still worried about Noella's potential to be unscrupulous in her approach to this issue but as she reflected on her career, she decided she was really in the right place after all.

****

"Ms. Monahan, please come to the office," Lianna heard on the public address system in the hallway. She had just been to visit the Grade 1 classrooms and felt very positive about the high-quality teaching she had seen. She decided not to rush, but she knew that when she got called to the office, there must be something important.

Patricia looked worried when Lianna came into the office. "Ms. Lianna, there is a lawyer on line 3 and he says that if you don't take the call, you'd regret it. I am fed up with people's threats and I told him that you might be busy. I thought I should let you know. Do you want to take the call or should I take a message for you?"

"Once again, I'm so sorry you have to deal with stuff like this Patricia!

I really am!" Lianna said sympathetically to the best assistant she'd ever had. "You really deserve to be paid more! I'll take the call and thanks again!"

"It's all part of the job, Miss," said Patricia. Lianna went into her office, closed the door and again she gathered her thoughts and took a deep breath before she picked up the call.

"Lianna Monahan speaking," she said with confidence as she sat down in her office chair. She wondered what Noella had now cooked up and what sordid things this lawyer was going to say this time.

"Ms. Monahan, my name is Jack Albany and I represent Noella De Haviland."

"Ok," replied Lianna.

Ms. De Haviland is quite upset that you've sent an email out to your school community; an email that directly attacks her integrity I might add. She is contemplating a law suit against you for defamation of character. Do you have any response before I file the papers?" he stated very matter-of-factly.

Lianna was beginning to develop a deep disdain for lawyers although she knew she shouldn't paint them all with the same brush. She paused for a moment to contemplate her next response.

"Well, Mr. Albany," Lianna began, "I have very little comment for you other than the fact that what I've sent to the community is the truth, unlike what Ms. De Havilland's message conveyed to them. She also chose to leave out important information about the situation and her message instilled some fear in *my* clients. I suppose I could have them launch a class action suit against Noella for instilling fear using false information and sending a message that I (the person in charge of this school's communication) most certainly didn't approve. So ... here's what I recommend to you Mr. Albany ... please tell Ms. De Havilland that should she continue to distribute propaganda to my parents via email, that the board lawyers will certainly and unequivocally send her a cease-and-desist order! And *THAT,* Mr. Albany .... is my response! Good day!" and with that Lianna hung up the phone.

Man, that felt good, she thought. She was proud of the way she handled the situation.

Lianna continued with her usual work for the rest of the day, then decided to go home early. She needed to see her girls, who she hadn't talked to very much in the past few days. As she entered the condo, Alfred was there to greet her. "So nice to see you, Lianna! How was your day?

"Thank you, Alfred. It was a more difficult day than usual, but it ended on a good note. How are you doing?" Lianna asked sincerely.

"Very good, thank you Miss," he replied. "The girls came home about a half hour ago." He added. "I think they are looking forward to seeing you." This made Lianna feel great, and she couldn't wait to see them.

She made her way to the elevator and then pushed the button for the 34th floor. The ride up was fast as usual. Lianna made her way down the hall and to the left where her condo door was situated. She swiped her fob and entered her place. The girls were together sitting on the sofa and they suddenly became very quiet. Lianna was curious.

"Hi girls. How was the week with your dad?" she asked with great interest.

The girls looked at each other in a bit of a strange way, then Diane decided to speak first.

"Pretty good," Diane replied. "But I think we should probably ask you how your week was." Diane had a playful sound in her voice which implied to Lianna that they suspected something. Lianna wondered if they knew about her latest overnight guest.

"Honestly, this was a very hard week, girls. I've had lawyers calling me and difficult parents trying to spoil my reputation, but other than that it was pretty good," Lianna explained.

"Are you sure there's nothing else you'd like to tell us?" asked Dallas with a playfully suspicious tone of voice. Dallas was intuitive and suspected Lianna had spent a lot of time with Todd.

"Like what?" Lianna responded, thinking she might be *busted*. Lianna looked away and casually dropped her work bag by the kitchen island.

"Why won't you look at us?" Diane said with a slight giggle. Now Lianna knew they had some information that she couldn't hide.

"Alright!" Lianna exclaimed sheepishly. "Todd and I went on a dinner date and he was here for a while after!"

"What do you mean by a while?" Dallas probed more deeply, hoping her mother would just come out and admit it.

"A while," Lianna said again. "I guess I would mean ... more than twelve hours."

"Oooohhh!" the girls both responded, as if to tease their mother, because they knew exactly what that meant. "Are you going to see him again?" Diane asked, in a genuine tone. Lianna laughed, and was relieved that the girls didn't seem to be mad at her. She knew they both liked Todd as they had reached out to him about holding a party for their mom at their place.

"I think I might," Lianna said teasingly. She knew she would get a reaction from the girls and a second later Dallas responded.

"You *have* to Mom! He's the only decent guy you've ever known since Dad. You know we like him … we *really* like him!" Dallas was very clear in her words and she needed to let their mom know that in no uncertain terms …Todd had their seal of approval. Just then, Lianna's cell phone rang and so she answered it, not expecting the next voice she would hear.

Chapter 11

"Well…well…well… if it isn't the queen of scandal herself," said Noella on the other end of the phone. Noella's voice was upsetting to Lianna and she knew if she never heard it again, she'd be more than ok with that.

"Ahhh…just the person I least hoped to hear from right now!" said Lianna sarcastically. "To what do I owe this immense pleasure?"

Noella was quiet for a moment and then suddenly spoke. "You think you're so beyond litigation that you could threaten to get a cease-and-desist order against me? You must be dreaming MS. Monahan!" There was now anger in Noella's voice but Lianna was satisfied that she'd shaken her a little.

"And I dream in vivid colour, Noella." Lianna said, with a sarcastic tone. She was proud of standing up to this insensitive woman who only thought of herself. She also knew that the more she could push Noella's buttons the more likely it would throw her off her game … and in Lianna's mind it was now becoming a game.

"In that case," Noella began smugly, "Let me paint you a picture … in vivid colour." By now, Lianna was ready for anything Noella had to throw at her. She almost welcomed Noella's next words. "Are you ready to use your imagination Ms. Monahan?" Noella asked sarcastically.

"Bring it on, Noella," responded Lianna. There was silence on the phone for a moment then a louder voice from Noella could be heard.

"Alright …MS. Monahan! Here's what I see." said Noella. "In your future, I see debt. I see you paying out thousands of dollars in lawsuits for neglecting your school. So, I'm seeing the colour blue to match your despair.

I see red to match your anger ... anger at yourself for your own negligence and I see green as well. Do you want to know what that represents, Ms. Monahan?"

"I can't wait to hear this one!" said Lianna sarcastically.

"Green ..." Noella began with an evil tone of voice, "is for the envy you feel when you meet your replacement after being removed from the principal's chair."

"I see Noella," said Lianna. "And are there any other colours in your picture?"

"Only black," replied Noella. "Black represents the darkness of your heart as the gloom and doom permeates your soul." Noella sounded very proud of the picture she painted for Lianna.

Lianna could almost hear Noella cackling like a witch in a cartoon movie, and she started to imagine what that might look like.

"Well, Noella ..." Lianna carefully began her response, "You have certainly proven yourself to be a good painter. In fact, everything is quite clear and I have to give you a good grade on the picture. I just have to ask one question ..."

"And what would that be?" asked Noella. She was curious as to what she might hear.

"Did you wash your hands after?" Lianna curiously asked.

"What do you mean?" said Noella. "Why?"

"To get the paint off your fingers," Lianna responded seriously.

Noella laughed nervously. "Why would there be paint on my fingers?" she asked.

"It *is* a finger-painting isn't it, Noella? And I would hate for you to have touched anything afterwards. I know the kindergarten kids wash their hands when they're done, and I just assumed you would too." Lianna was now speaking with a very sarcastic tone of voice. She could almost feel Noella's anger through the phone.

"Well, I never!!!" Exclaimed Noella indignantly. "You're saying that my picture … is a … *finger-painting*?"

"Well, if the finger fits Noella …" Lianna replied sarcastically. "I can't see you right now but I can imagine which finger you'd be holding up."

Lianna smiled to herself and chuckled in a defiant way. "And if I may say so … I'd guess that since your husband left you, that finger has probably come in handy on more than one occasion." Lianna wondered whether she'd crossed the line with that comment but Noella had just been cruel with the colour metaphor and Lianna wasn't about to be abused.

"You're going to be sorry you had this conversation Ms. Monaghan," Noella said with anger. "You'll be hearing from my lawyer again!" she added.

"Oh … like last time?" Lianna asked her sarcastically. Lianna was again trying to show Noella that she wouldn't pushed around. By this time Noella was extremely frustrated and she hung up the phone without saying anything more. Lianna wasn't worried about this in the least and in fact was quite proud that she'd pushed Noella to this point.

Lianna turned back to her daughters and said, "You see? That's how you handle bullies!"

Both the girls started clapping, wanting their mother to know they were very proud of how she handled the call.

"What is that parent doing calling you at home anyway?" Dallas asked. Lianna thought for a moment and finally said, "I'm not really sure …" and looked at Dallas like she had made an excellent point.

Her daughter knew very well that Noella shouldn't be calling her mom and especially making threats or being abusive on the phone.

"Dallas …you are absolutely, 100 percent correct! I don't know why I'd even pick up the call. I guess I know what to do next time, right?" Lianna affirmed her daughter's point of view, making Dallas feel good about defending her mom. Dallas was also very astute when it came to social relationships and her mother knew this.

"I'm making dinner tonight," announced Diane. "After all, I am the older daughter …and the better chef!" she stated boastfully and looked at Dallas with a teasing sort of look.

"In your dreams!" Dallas responded, disagreeing very much with her older sister. *At least they were still talking* thought Lianna, and that was a good sign.

The three of them had a delicious supper prepared by Diane and Lianna so very much appreciated the effort. She was grateful for both her daughters and knew she had done a good job of raising them. She worried about them all the time as any mother would, but in her heart, she knew they would be ok.

Web of Lies

****

Meanwhile, Noella had called the school board offices and wanted to speak with the chief superintendent. "Yes, Ms. De Havilland," said Brad.

"I realize that your lawyer is asking for a full investigation into our procedures about asbestos in our schools. I assure you we have taken every possible step to ensure that our buildings are safe for children. They wouldn't be allowed in the building if we hadn't done that."

"Well Mr. Croskenheimer, I know you *say* that, but it's one thing to say it and another thing to *do* it. One of your former employees, doesn't believe you've kept up with regular checks to ensure that nothing has been disturbed in walls or other places that contain asbestos." Noella was doubtful that Brad had taken action.

"I now have copies of reports that show that the last inspection of Viscount Elton School was more than 15 years ago. How do you respond to that?" Noella questioned with a sarcastic tone.

"Until I've examined the reports myself, I'm going to have to reserve comment Ms. De Havilland," responded Brad. "I think from this point on, you will need to contact our lawyers if you want answers to your questions."

"So, you're afraid of direct conversation, Mr. Croskenheimer?" Noella asked in a skeptical tone of voice.

"Absolutely not," Brad responded. "But I think we've reached a point where you're grasping at straws to find answers that you might twist in your favour. Our lawyers have advised me that once we reach that point, I should refer you to them. So, I'm taking the advice of counsel."

"That's unfortunate," said Noella.

"I thought you were a man of integrity who truly listened to parents. I guess you're not the man I thought you were Mr. Croskenheimer."

"Mam, I assure you that I have the best interests of the children in everything I do. As for integrity, I assure you that nothing is more important in my work. Once you question that, Ms. De Haviland, you have reached that point where I must end our conversation. Good day to you!"

And with that, Brad ended the call. He was certainly finding out what it was like to deal directly with this difficult woman, and he wasn't impressed with her tactics. It was now time to ramp up their legal defense against this woman who was trying to satisfy personal need for power and control.

Chapter 12

Lianna went into the school feeling refreshed after a great night with her daughters. She felt more in control of her situation and that she had the full support of her bosses. Teachers and support staff were continually stopping by to reassure her that she was the best principal they'd ever worked for and they made her feel confident and satisfied that she was doing a great job. They also expressed their anger that Noella was causing problems for the school and hoped that Lianna was doing ok.

"I just can't believe she has the audacity to accuse you of wrong doing!" said Deana Jackson, a veteran teacher who'd been at the school for 21 years. "I've seen some tough parents in my time here, but never like this one!" They chatted for a couple minutes, then the first bell rang to signal the entry of students.

"Thanks so much!" Lianna said. "I appreciate your comments. But please excuse me … I have to get to the doors to greet students which is always the best part of my morning." With that, Lianna excused herself and headed for the main doors where students were beginning to file in.

She repeated her usual greetings as one by one they entered the school with smiling faces. This truly *was* the best part of her job. Seeing the smiles on the faces of all her students was worth all the challenges she faced, and it reminded her how lucky she was to be a principal. What would she do without all those smiles and laughter in the children each and every day?

The school day began and went forward with no trouble. Lianna got caught up on some of her reports and even had time to briefly visit each classroom. This reinforced that she was in the best school in the city …

exactly where she needed to be. It also reminded her that she needed to fight hard for the students against anyone who wanted to take away their school. She was now a warrior for their cause and she didn't take this lightly.

Lianna was indeed a warrior when it came to advocating for kids. She also was an advocate for her staff and defended them on many occasions. As a single parent she had to be tough, standing up for herself with her ex-husband but also standing up for the kids and their needs.

In short, she had no choice but to be strong and resilient.

She had a difficult upbringing with an absent father and a mother who was mentally and physically challenged. They didn't have much money and grew up without many luxuries. Her grandfather provided what he could on a meagre salary; the basics were always there but no extras. She wore very plain clothes and at times was teased as a "poor" child. Overall, she managed to come out ahead in spite of many challenges as a young person.

"Call for you on line one, Ms. Lianna." said Patricia. "I don't know who it is and they wouldn't say when I asked for a name. Lianna was cautious as she moved toward her phone.

"Lianna Monahan speaking," she said with a confident voice. "How can I help you?" She was hesitant to hear the next voice in her ear.

"Ms. Monahan, how are you today?" said a familiar voice and she was relieved to hear it was Todd's.

"Oh, thank God, Todd! It's you!" she said with relief in her voice. "I was worried it was another lawyer calling me with more bad news."

"I get it," said Todd with understanding. "I can't blame you for your reaction. So, are we on for this weekend?"

Todd was excited for the possibilities ahead for the two of them as a couple. "I don't want to pressure you Lianna, you know that, right?"

"No pressure at all Todd," she responded with a loving voice. She knew she wanted to see him again soon, and couldn't wait for the weekend. "I've practically got my overnight bag packed already," she added.

"That's the best news I've had all week," said Todd. "Shall I pick you up, or do you want to drive to my place?"

"I should probably bring my car," said Lianna. "In case there's an emergency at home with the girls. They're old enough to be on their own for a couple days and I trust them … I just need to be able to respond quickly and on a moment's notice if anything goes crazy."

"That makes total sense," answered Todd understandingly. "So, Friday night dinner at my place?" he asked. "I'm making a delectable dish I've perfected over the years, and I think you're going to love it!"

"Can't wait." Lianna responded. "What time Friday?"

"Shall we say, 7:00 P.M.?" said Todd. "That should give you a chance to fix supper for your girls before you leave."

"Sounds perfect … and Todd …" Lianna quietly exclaimed.

"Yes Lianna?"

"I'm not bringing pajamas … but I am bringing my toothbrush," said Lianna seductively.

Todd laughed an understanding laugh. Just then another call was coming in on Lianna's cell phone. "I think I should take this call, Todd. The number is blocked but it could be one of the girls."

"No problem, Lianna. I'll see you Friday night…in no pajamas." He laughed again. Lianna said goodbye and picked up the call on her cell phone.

"Hello," she said. There was silence on the other end for a moment, then a male voice spoke.

"Is this Lianna Monahan?" the mysterious voice asked.

"That depends …who wants to know?" Lianna asked proceeding with caution.

"My name is Joe and I have information you might like to hear. Is this line recorded for quality assurance purposes?" he tried to joke. Lianna just laughed and responded.

"I'm afraid it's just the two of us Joe. Do you have a last name?" Lianna probed, hoping to identify the caller a little better.

"Joe is all you need to know," the caller responded quietly. "I hear you're having some trouble with a certain parent in your school." Lianna was very concerned about a stranger knowing this and now needed to know more. And how did he get her cell number?

"OK …Joe. Why would I need to know what you have to tell me?" Lianna was extremely curious by now.

"It involves a bonus paid to Ms. De Havilland when she was on city council," Joe stated. "It appears that there were some kickbacks to certain council members who prioritized contracts for different companies in the city. Do you want to hear more, Ms. Monahan?" Joe added.

"I'm certainly curious, Joe," Lianna said with anticipation.

"I have a phone number and a person for you to contact. Do you want it?" Joe asked.

"Absolutely, Joe…" said Lianna. The wheels of justice were starting to turn in her mind as she envisioned catching Noella in a scandal. Actually, the wheels of revenge became the new justice for her as she eagerly awaited the name and number.

"Do you have a pen and paper, Lianna?"

"Absolutely! I'm ready … fire away!"

"Your contact's name is Monique… and her number is (929) 417-3666," Joe carefully stated. "Do you want to repeat that back to me, Lianna?

"Ok let's see, Joe … I've got Monique at (929) 417-3666 is that right?"

"You got it right, Lianna. But don't leave it too long before you call her." Joe had an urgency in his voice which told Lianna he meant business. "She has limited access to the documents and you don't want to miss your window of opportunity."

"Thank you, Joe. Will I hear from you again or can I contact you again?" Lianna asked, hopeful she could track down Joe if needed.

"I'm afraid not," Joe said. "It's too dangerous for me. The people I'm dealing with wouldn't like that very much and to be honest, Lianna, you're dealing with one crazy lady with some … let us say *scary* connections in this city. So, my advice to you is … be *very* careful!"

"Thank you, Joe," Lianna responded. "You seem like a decent man and I greatly appreciate the advice."

"All in a day's work for me, Lianna. Oh… and one more thing … be cautious of a man named Mitch. That's all I can say. I wish you the best!" Joe stated with a sincere tone that made Lianna feel she could trust him.

"Thank you again, Joe. Have a wonderful day!" Lianna replied and then ended the call. She decided to take a moment to absorb and process what just happened. She almost couldn't believe that the call was real and wondered what would happen if she called the number. Was it a trap set by Noella to catch Lianna in a breach of privacy? Would Noella then be able to use this as further ammunition to oust her from the school. It was certainly something she had to think about and decided she would get Todd's advice this weekend. After all, it was Thursday and in less than 36 hours, she would be with Todd once again.

****

Friday night came quickly after a good day at the school. Lianna rushed home from work, had a shower, then prepared a pasta dinner for the girls. They came home late from school but Lianna kept the food warm in the oven.

She then went to put on her make-up and choose a sexy outfit for the evening and finish packing her overnight bag.

She could hardly contain her excitement as she imagined the weekend ahead with Todd, and there were moments where her body actually felt the heat of passion that she so desperately needed from him right now.

Dallas and Diane arrived home together and as soon as they came in, they smelled the wonderful aroma of the pasta sauce and garlic bread waiting for them.

"Something smells absolutely delicious," said Diane as they put their backpacks away in the mud room. "Mom, are you here?" she called out.

Lianna came out of her bedroom in a stunning black dress and stiletto heels, looking like a million dollars. The girls were both amazed at how their mother looked, and they hadn't seen her look that good for some time.

"OMG!" said Dallas, as they both stared at their mom in disbelief. "You look amazing, mom!"

"Why, thank you," responded Lianna. "I think I'm ready for a great weekend. Are you girls ready for an amazing pasta meal?"

"More than ready!" exclaimed Diane as they headed toward the kitchen area to see what was in the oven. "Mmmmm … this is going to taste delicious!"

"I think you'll enjoy it," said Lianna as she looked for her car keys. "I wanted to cook you two at least one meal this weekend. Maybe there will be enough for leftovers one night."

Lianna felt a little guilty about leaving them alone, but she knew they understood. They also really liked Todd and wanted to see their mom with a decent guy.

"All good Mom," reassured Dallas. "We're old enough to look after ourselves and … we are not going to starve ourselves. We know how to cook a thing or two."

"Yes …Dallas has now learned how to boil water!" said Diane teasing her sister once again. She looked at Dallas who scowled at her as she got plates out of the cupboard.

"Go and have a great weekend with Todd, Mom," said Diane with empathy in her voice and she gently touched Lianna's shoulder. Lianna gave her a hug then went over to Dallas who already had her arms outstretched.

"I'm so lucky to have the two of you!" she said to them almost with tears in her eyes. "At least two good things came from my marriage to your dad!"

"Thanks mom," Dallas and Diane said almost simultaneously. "Now *GO!*" added Diane.

"I'll be home for supper on Sunday," Lianna explained. "Maybe we can bring in a pizza and watch a movie or something." Lianna moved toward the door and said, "Are you girls sure you'll be ok?"

"*GO!*" The girls firmly said to their mother at the same time.

"See you Sunday. And call me any time if you need me," Lianna said reassuringly. With that, she opened the door and headed out for what would no doubt be an amazing weekend.

Chapter 13

Lianna pulled up at Todd's condo and called him from down below. She was nervous with excitement and hoped he felt the same.

"Hey Todd. I'm down below. Can I park underground in visitor parking?"

"Oh, I'm so sorry Lianna. Yes, I need to give you the code. It's 2478, and my stall is F13," Todd said apologetically. "Then just head to the left to find the elevators when you're down there. You know my unit number, right?

"I think it's 2842 … am I right?" Lianna asked.

"You got it! Come on up," said Todd with much anticipation. He was quite nervous, but also happy that Lianna had agreed to come. While he waited, he poured champaign in two glasses and lit several candles to enhance the romantic mood. Dinner was in the oven, and he had prepared the delicious meal with care and precision. He was ready for the evening, the fireplace glowing in the living room with dim lights throughout the main area.

Lianna entered the code carefully and drove to the underground visitor parking stalls. Her heart beat rapidly as she thought about the possibilities ahead. She got out of the car, grabbed her overnight bag, and headed toward the elevators.

She stopped at the main floor as she had to catch another elevator before going up to Todd's place. The concierge greeted her with a friendly smile and she made her way into the elevator before heading up to the 28th floor.

Again, she felt her heart racing as she watched the elevator floor numbers one floor at a time getting her closer and closer to Todd's. By the time she hit the 28th floor she felt like her heart would pop out of her chest with anticipation. The door opened and she stepped out to the left walking 4 doors down the hallway toward Todd's place. She reached his door and knocked quietly, wondering if he would hear. Suddenly the door opened slowly and Todd's smiling face was there to greet her. She felt her heart melt as he gestured for her to come inside.

He spoke not a word, but took her bag and motioned over to the couch, where she saw the glasses of champaign and the candles burning softly on the table. The room was dimly lit to accentuate the romance Todd created for them.

"You've really thought this through carefully, Todd," Lianna said, as she took a sip of her drink. "Mmmm ... this is spectacular champaign. What brand is it?"

"Chateau LeFrenue," Todd replied. "2015 ... it was a good year for them."

"It's wonderful," Lianna said as she looked into his eyes with a knowing look that made Todd melt. She held eye contact with him for what seemed like a long time, then she spoke. "So how are you tonight, Todd? How was your week?"

"I'd rather talk about better things like you and me," Todd responded, not wanting to engage in shop talk. He knew they would just end up talking about Noella, and that would spoil the evening. Todd noticed that Lianna had finished most of her glass of champaign so he offered her more. "You must be thirsty," he laughed as he held the bottle over her glass. She responded with a head nod of approval and he filled her glass. He knew she was nervous and probably just needed to calm her nerves a bit so he understood. He was nervous too but wanted it to be a perfect night for both of them.

They continued to sip on their champaign and soon Todd asked Lianna if she was hungry to which she replied yes. He invited her to the dining area table that was beautifully set with fancy napkins, wine glasses and candles and an exquisite center piece of flowers consisting of roses and lilies. He brought the food to the table, starting with a lovely Caesar salad with fresh croutons, and just the right amount of dressing which included a little Dijon mustard and lots of garlic.

"This is one of my specialties, Lianna." Todd explained as he served her the salad on her plate. "My Nona's recipe which has been in the family for generations. Every time I make it, I make it with love as I think of her and her dedication to our family."

"Looks … and smells wonderful, Todd," Lianna responded as she waited for him to serve himself. "I can't wait to try it!"

"All right!" Todd said, as he signaled to Lianna that they should dig in and enjoy.

"Oh…my…God! This is amazing, Todd!" exclaimed Lianna who was so impressed with the salad.

She took a few more bites and all the time she almost hummed with delight with every fork full. "You certainly know how to make an amazing Caesar," Lianna said as she continued to savor bite after bite.

"As I said," Todd responded humbly, "It's one of my specialties." He continued to look at her with loving eyes and she knew he was thinking of the time they would spend. She couldn't wait to make love to him once again, and her instinctual self almost wished they could skip dinner and go straight to bed. She caught herself before she made the day dream obvious with him and decided to talk.

"I'm so happy here with you, Todd," Lianna explained. "I feel very lucky to be with a man as amazing and successful as you."

She lifted her glass toward him and said, "I'd like to propose a toast …".

Todd responded by lifting his glass in the air and she continued. "To friendship and love, and to the amazing times yet to be experienced."

"To friendship and our love," Todd said sweetly, as Lianna's feelings were confirmed. They drank from their glasses then finished their salads then Todd collected the salad plates to clear the table for the main course.

He brought out the next course which was a chicken Cordon Bleu with an amazing Italian sauce over top. There were delicious dinner rolls with butter which Lianna really loved. She had a weakness for bread and Todd knew it.

They continued to enjoy the food, then indulged in a dessert that Todd also made from scratch. It was a chocolate mousse with an amazing topping that melted in Lianna's mouth. She could not believe what a talented guy he was; smart, funny, successful, sensitive, a great leader, and an amazing cook to top it all off. She certainly hit the jackpot.

The evening went on and they sat on his balcony in comfortable chairs looking up at the stars. After 2 hours or so, Todd decided to make another move and he gave her the most passionate kiss he ever gave any woman. Her heart and body melted as he pulled her close in the moonlight which shimmered in the warm evening sky.

She began to moan softly, as Todd ran his hands over her bare shoulders lightly caressing them with his fingertips.

He then took her face in both his hands as he kissed her more deeply, parting her lips with his tongue that ached for hers. They both knew what lay ahead, but both of them were afraid of making any move that would jeopardize their evening. He then reached around to touch her buttocks and gently pull her even closer as their tongues continued to entwine.

After another moment or two she looked him in the eyes with a sultry look and whispered "Do you want me again, Todd?"

He looked deep into her eyes and said yes. She then went a step further and asked, "How badly?"

Todd responded immediately and said, "More than anyone or anything else in this world!" And he pulled her even closer, their bodies almost grinding at the hips without them realizing.

He then picked Lianna up and carried her back into the condo, and over toward the fireplace he had lit before she arrived. On the floor was a bearskin rug, supported by an inconspicuous soft underlay beneath. He gently lowered her to the surface, all the time never breaking eye contact with her.

"I want you *so* badly, Todd," moaned Lianna as he continued to caress her. He then reached for the buttons on her dress and one by one, he carefully undid them to reveal a very sexy black bra beneath. He then gently pulled the dress downward toward her waist, and she tilted her head back.

He kissed her neck and every area in between that and her breasts, which now were begging for release. Todd found the hook and carefully released her heaving breasts from their captive clothing. He began to kiss her again, getting stronger with each movement and his lips made their way downward to her now erect nipples, which eagerly received his tongue.

He caressed each breast with passion and precision as Lianna threw her head backward to be pleasured even more by this amazing man. She grabbed his head in both her hands, as he gently nibbled on her now swollen nipples, turning her on more than she had ever been turned on before.

Todd was eager to remove the rest of her clothing but he knew that he should take his time to make her feel comfortable. He gazed into her eyes and quietly whispered to her, "I want you too, Lianna," and he gently tugged on her dress and moved it downward to her feet. He saw the sexy black G-string panties which nearly drove him over the edge, but he kept control and continued to remove the dress entirely.

Lianna was on her back, warm and cozy on the bearskin rug and Todd positioned his mouth over her navel and began kissing her soft skin, gently at first, then becoming more forceful as he strategically made his way closer to the top of her G-string. Her moaning became louder with every movement of his lips, and finally, he latched on with his teeth and slowly pulled then downward over her thighs, watching her as he did it. She knew what she wanted and so did he.

He took the panties over her ankles with his hand, all the while kissing between her thighs as she anticipated what was about to happen. She grabbed his head between her hands and pulled him closer to her. There was a drop of nectar coming from her cavern, which Todd could see, but he would tease her just a bit more before tasting the forbidden fruit.

Seconds seemed like hours to Lianna as she waited for him to commit his tongue to her womanhood. Finally, and without warning, she pulled his head onto her, throwing her head back in ecstasy as he explored her, gently at first, then with more force. She held tight, still letting him move his head the way he wanted, but kept him close. She never wanted him to stop.

Suddenly, also without warning, she yelled out, "Yes!", as she reached her peak. She held his head even more firmly, while wave after wave of pleasure consumed her entire body. It was almost like a dream in slow motion as Todd ensured that she was fully satisfied.

Lianna then unbuttoned Todd's shirt and nearly tore it from his manly torso. She reached down frantically unbuttoning his jeans which were now fully expanded with his impending excitement.

Todd knew he had to give her what she needed, and he helped her by removing his pants. He kneeled before her; his boxers full of his manhood waiting to be released. Lianna moved her head closer and grabbed the top of them with her teeth and slowly removed them from his legs.

"I need you now Todd," Lianna exclaimed, as she lay back and motioned to him to come over top of her. Todd eagerly complied, and soon his manhood was close to her waiting cavern. "Please Todd!"

 Lianna moaned, and with that he plunged deep into her being, keeping eye contact with her and grasping each hand with his own. Lianna moved her hands over her head and Todd followed suit. It was almost as if she wanted him to dominate her with gentle control.

He started slowly thrusting in and out, back and forth, with his manhood exploring as much of her cavern as possible. She rhythmically met his thrusts with her own, grinding her pelvis against him faster and stronger with every move. Todd felt his excitement building, and as Lianna approached her peak and moaned even louder, Todd tried to hold himself back.

Soon, it was too late for both of them and they simultaneously succumbed to their instincts, collapsing together when the pleasure subsided. They held each other close, gazing into each other's eyes until they fell asleep, each of them satisfied and certain they were deeply in love.

Chapter 14

The morning light seemed to come quickly as they woke up still holding each other. Todd was certain that Lianna was the woman he wanted to meet for a very long time. Lianna was also certain that there was no one else in this world that would ever be like Todd, and so it was that their deep love for each other began.

They spent the day in bed, just talking about their dreams and how they each saw the relationship unfolding. There was, of course, the matter of their teenage kids that they needed to discuss, and how to tell them about their serious relationship. Neither of them seemed too worried about how the kids would take the news, as both families were somewhat familiar with the other person.

"Let's watch a movie tonight," Lianna said as they were sitting in the living room talking.

"Sounds great," said Todd. "What kind of movies do you like?"

"Chick Flicks," said Lianna playfully, as she looked through the Netflix listings to find a romance. Todd laughed, and rolled his eyes pretending to be unenthused about her choice but the truth was ... he liked romance movies as well.

"While I'm thinking of it, there is one thing I need to run by you, Todd," said Lianna with hesitation.

"Uh oh!" replied Todd, a bit worried she had bad news or something. "Is my condo too messy or something? Or maybe the bath towels are not soft enough for you?" He laughed as he looked her in the eyes, teasing her a bit.

"I'm serious, Todd," Lianna explained as she gave him a gentle love slap on the knee. "I got a very strange call a couple days ago."

"Who from?" Todd asked.

"Well, that's just it," Lianna responded, "I'm not really sure who they are ... I only know they have access to information about Noella's time on City Council. They said if I call someone named Monique, they'd give me inside information about Noella taking bribes from companies to award them contracts."

"And you don't know who the caller was?" asked Todd skeptically. "Maybe it's a set-up by Noella ... putting some bate out for you to grab onto thinking you're going to catch her?"

"Well, that thought did cross my mind," said Lianna. "I know I need to be careful, but they seemed to say that I would get some solid evidence of wrong doing on Noella's part and that it might help my situation. The man seemed very sincere and I got the impression that they know someone who doesn't like Noella very much. They said it was too dangerous for them to call me back again, only that I should call Monique at the city offices."

"I see," said Todd. "So, what do you think you'll do?"

"It won't hurt for me to hear them out," said Lianna. "It might be just what we need to discredit Noella with the board and the trustees."

"You have a good point there," Todd said.

"There's definite risk involved in terms of privacy and where you obtain any documents to prove any conflict of interest, but overall, I think it's a risk worth taking."

"Thanks Todd. I really appreciate and respect your opinion. You're the smartest guy…" she paused for a few seconds then added, "in the room!" Lianna joked playfully and Todd laughed at her humor which reminded him of "dad" jokes.

"There is hope for your comedy career yet," Todd responded. "Especially when your career as a principal is done." They both laughed together and Lianna continued her search for a movie in the Netflix listings.

"How about this one?" Lianna asked him as she pointed to the movie titled 'Passionate Summer on Santorini'.

"Actually, I love movies set in the Greek Islands," said Todd enthusiastically. "They take my mind far away, and it's almost like going on vacation!"

"Passionate Summer it is," said Lianna confirming their decision. "See Todd, that wasn't so hard … we make good decisions together!"

"We'll see!" Todd laughed. "I'll let you know how good it was in 90 minutes from now. They both smiled at each other, reminded of how good they were together.

They watched the movie, having popcorn and chocolate bars that Todd had bought just for the occasion, and when it was time, they retired for the night, both somewhat exhausted not only from the night before but also the week that led up to this. They fell asleep in each other's arms once again.

Sunday came around, and they decided to go for a lovely breakfast at the Riverside Cafe, enjoying the sunshine as they ate. They talked more about their kids and tried to avoid talking about work as much as possible.

Lianna was surprised she didn't get a call from Dallas who always had a little separation anxiety when away from her mother. Were the girls up to no good back at home?

Did they have a wild party with boys in the house last night? Her imagination wandered to a few different scenarios but in the end, her common sense prevailed as did her trust in her daughters.

"So, we need to get our families together," Lianna said to Todd. I am certain that the girls will enjoy your boys and vice versa …if Diane doesn't try to show her attitude of superior intelligence. She has a tendency to talk down to boys sometimes as if she knows more and pretends to be way more mature.

I think your boys have good heads on their shoulders and I think they'll be able to tolerate her attitude when it comes right down to it. Maybe just give them a heads up about Diane. Dallas will be no problem."

"I think it will be great!" said Todd. "What shall we do with them?"

"Well…I thought about an escape room, but then I didn't want Diane to be too assertive especially when solving clues to get out. I also thought about a bike ride or even going bowling which might be fun. Do you want to ask the boys what they'd prefer?"

"Sure. I think that would be a great idea." Todd responded. "If they have some choice it won't seem like a chore to them."

"That makes sense," replied Lianna. "Maybe give us a few days heads up. Then I can prepare the girls." She smiled at Todd who agreed with a knowing wink and a nod. He knew the boys would love Diane's girls and felt good about their plan.

"Speaking of bike rides, would you like to join me on one today?" asked Todd. "I have two bikes and a rack on my car. We can go anywhere you'd like Lianna." Todd offered her the choice knowing she enjoyed cycling and hoped she would go with him.

"Ok. How about … Canmore?" Lianna replied enthusiastically.

"Done!" Todd responded eagerly. They went back to his condo and changed into some biking clothes, then loaded the bikes on the rack attached to Todd's Toyota 4 Runner. Lianna not only loved this vehicle and felt safe in it, but she also enjoyed the scenic drive out to the mountains.

They had a wonderful afternoon in Canmore, seeing some amazing and picturesque sites as they rode the bike trails. They were both quite fit, and so riding the bikes was not difficult for either of them except for some uphill rides in various locations. Lianna would occasionally speed past Todd and entice him to ride faster, which he did. They thoroughly enjoyed the ride together, stopping on occasion to take pictures of the mountain scenery as well as each other. On the way back, they stopped for tacos, before heading back to Todd's where Lianna gathered her things and prepared to go home to her girls.

"Did you enjoy the weekend?" asked Todd, as he put his arms around her at the door.

"It was best weekend I've had in longer than I can remember," Lianna replied. Todd was sorry to have to say goodbye and wished she could stay there for a while. He knew her girls needed her and he also needed to catch up with his boys, who would soon return from sleepovers at their friends' places.

"Glad to hear that," said Todd, thinking that seeing her again wouldn't come soon enough.

"It was truly amazing for me, Lianna. I am so much in love with you, I can't begin to describe it. Todd reached out and gently held her face in both hands and kissed her passionately. Lianna responded in kind, and they held each other close for several minutes.

"Well ... I should go now." Lianna explained.

"I'll walk you down to your car, babe," Todd said as he opened the door. Together they took the elevator, both looking at the floors as it slowly approached the underground parking. The doors opened and Lianna headed in the direction of her car.

"You know I'm going to miss you this week, don't you?" she said to Todd.

"Not as much as I'll miss you my angel," replied Todd and soon they arrived at her car. "We're going to have to talk on the phone ... a lot!"

"I agree," she said as she put her bag in the back seat. "Every day as a matter of fact."

"I'm going to hold you to it," said Todd as he kissed and hugged her one more time.

"Looking forward to it," she said as she quickly got behind the wheel.

"I love you, Todd." With that she pulled away leaving his heart feeling full of joy, but empty because they had to part company for a few days. It was truly a weekend to remember.

****

Lianna arrived home after a thoughtful drive, and she couldn't stop thinking about Todd. No matter what she tried to do to distract herself or get him out of her mind … she couldn't.

She passed through the lobby and was greeted by Alfred who asked her how the weekend went. She smiled and said it couldn't have been better. Returning a knowing smile Alfred responded, "Your girls were very good. No boys going in and out of here so I guess you can be pleased about that."

Lianna laughed. "You are absolutely right Alfred," she said to him. "As usual."

Lianna took the elevator up to her floor and as she exited toward her unit, she heard loud music from down the hall. She was ready to scold her daughters for playing music too loud, but as she got closer, she realized that it was the neighbor next door to them that had cranked their stereo … not Dallas and Diane. Lianna felt bad for thinking this way, and soon entered her condo to find the girls seated at the dining table, a gourmet-like meal in front of them and no company per se.

"Hungry Mom?" said Diane, who was grinning from ear to ear. Dallas also looked at her mother grinning widely and she had a bit of a flushed looked on her cheeks, as if she was embarrassed for her mom.

"To be truthful girls," Lianna began, "I had tacos on the way home from biking in Canmore. But I'd love to try your cooking!"

"Hate to disappoint, Mom, but we got this food from the neighbors … the Galloways down the hall." The girls were laughing and soon their mother broke out in laughter as well.

"Well, I can see you survived just fine," Lianna stated. She was proud of her girls for taking care of themselves … even if someone else did the cooking.

Chapter 15

Lianna arrived at school the next day to see a large yellow envelope on her desk. She saw the label in the corner which read "Court of King's Bench" and she knew what had to be inside. Normally, this would have upset her to some degree but right now, nothing surprised her.

There was a bit of a buzz in the office, with teachers coming in and out and the phones were ringing off the hook. Karen, a Grade 5 teacher, came by to say good morning and to ask Lianna if she could leave early for a medical appointment. Lianna obliged, saying she would dismiss Karen's students at the end of the day.

Lianna was a good principal as well as a compassionate mentor and friend. But she also knew where to draw the line when it came to socializing with her staff, and was very professional about that. Karen had been a friend of hers even before Lianna became a principal, so they still socialized outside the school environment. Lianna always felt that the more she did for her staff, the more they would be there for her when she needed support.

Lianna opened the envelope carefully and confirmed that it was a subpoena to appear in court for accusations of negligence. She knew she'd have to call Brad, but set it aside to do her morning routine with the students as they came in the doors.

After everyone was settled in classrooms, Lianna headed back to the office to find Chief Brad, Deputy Chas, Board chair Richard Hammond and one other man she didn't recognize waiting for her to return.

"Good morning Lianna," said Brad cheerfully. "Sorry to arrive unannounced, but we're hoping to chat for a few minutes. Do you have time?"

"I always have time for you Brad. You know that!" Lianna said cheerfully but trying to hide her anxiety about the subpoena. "Do you want to meet in my office or in the conference room? We might have more room to spread out in the conference area."

Brad turned to Darren Matishyn, the Board's lawyer and said, "Darren this is Lianna Monahan, have you met each other?"

"No," said Darren. "Pleasure to meet you!"

"Likewise," said Lianna, as she shook his hand. "I suppose they've filled you in on what's been happening?"

"Yes … I'm afraid they have. So sorry this woman is putting you through this," Darren empathetically replied.

"It's part of the job sometimes," said Lianna, as she led them toward the conference room.

"I just got a subpoena from Noella's lawyers to appear for a civil trial in Court of King's Bench. It starts in 2 weeks from now. Is that reasonable?"

"Absolutely not! We'll ask for more time to prepare for the case," Darren assured her as they all sat down and closed the door. Brad looked very concerned, as did Chas, but they were happy to hear that Darren would push for a new trial date.

"So where do you think we stand Darren?" asked Brad who only briefly filled Darren in on the circumstances.

"It may be too early to tell until I see the evidence they're bringing forward. If they're just using the district's maintenance reports, then we are fully in compliance. If there's an outside inspection or any other information that seems to indicate liability, then we may need further ammunition to fight her on this." Darren wanted to be absolutely clear as he answered Brad, so there could be no misunderstanding. "Are you aware of any independent assessments of the asbestos in the building Brad?"

"Not that I'm aware but I'll check with Mitch Mason in the maintenance department to see if anything else might be on file," Brad responded.

"Sorry Brad. Did you say Mitch Mason?" Lianna thought about what Joe said about Mitch and was starting to feel a little more anxious about the whole thing.

"Don't worry Lianna. This is *not* on you!" Chas reassured her. "If there was an independent assessment, it would have been before your time at Carlton. It's more Mitch Mason's responsibility to keep on top of all of those inspection reports and stay up to date on any changes to the building."

"That's what I'm worried about. It just seems like Noella wouldn't be coming after me if she knew I held no responsibility. I think she knows something we don't," said Lianna nervously. "Maybe it has something to do with Mitch."

They all sat in silence for what seemed like an eternity to Lianna. They wondered what, if anything, Noella knew that could tip the scale in her favour and cause a problem for Lianna or the Board. Had Noella possibly altered documents to suit her case? In other words, forgery?

If she had done it when she worked for the city, maybe she would do it again. Lianna remembered the words of the caller 'Joe' and how he felt it was too dangerous to call Lianna or have her call him again. She began to think that there may have been other forces behind Noella that no one was aware of. Could she herself, be in danger if she called Monique?

"There's something I need to tell you all about," said Lianna hesitantly. "I received a phone call last week from a male caller named Joe. He gave me …" At that moment, the door to the conference room burst open and in stormed Noella, who was exceptionally angry.

"All right MS. Monahan! This time you've gone too far!" Noella began, raising her voice to an unreasonable level. "I tell you I'm not going to stand for this anymore! You've crossed the line with me by sending *thugs* to personally threaten my safety. They showed up at my door last night and told me I better back off or I may have an unfortunate *accident* in the near future.

I've given camera footage to the police and it's just a matter of time until they connect them to you!

You think you're so high and mighty that you can't be touched…but I tell you this…Once they prove you hired these people to threaten me, you'll be heading to jail and I am sure they will throw away the key. You can't get away with this …and you won't!"

"Please lower your voice, Ms. De Havilland," said Brad. "I assure you that Lianna would never ever do anything to threaten anyone!"

"Well, she did!" yelled Noella. "I don't know how she knows these people but I'd be worried if I were you. They were nothing short of mobsters working for a crime boss!"

"I assure you I had nothing to do with this, Noella," said Lianna calmly. "I wouldn't even know where to begin finding people who *could* threaten anyone!"

"Obviously someone else is unhappy with you Ms. De Havilland," said

Richard Hammond. "I believe Lianna and she would never ever do anything like this. It's absurd!"

"Obviously, she's pulled the wool over your eyes and fooled you all into thinking she's an angel who can do no wrong," Noella screamed. "You're all just as bad and I'm going to make sure you *all* go down for this. If not to jail…then hopefully out of a job for good! I'll be taking this to the media as soon as I gather my thoughts. You are all done! *DONE*! Do you hear me?" And with that she stormed out of the room as quickly and violently as she arrived.

"WOW! Can you believe that woman?" Chas said in disbelief. "She's off her rocker and she's losing all credibility by barging into meetings like that."

"Personally, I'm getting concerned about my own safety," said Lianna. "If these guys can threaten Noella who has great power and money in this city, what could they potentially do to people like ourselves?" Lianna was beginning to question whether she should follow up on Joe's information and call Monique to get more dirt on Noella. She figured she better tell Brad and the others at the table about her phone call from Joe.

"Before Noella stormed into the room, I was about to tell you about the call I got last week from a caller named Joe." Lianna stopped and took a breath before continuing. "He told me that his contact at the city offices had hard evidence that Noella was involved in accepting bribes from companies to award them contracts. When I asked him for a full name or a contact number to call him back, he refused and said it was too dangerous and he would only contact me once. He also said that a contact at the city named Monique only had a short window to access documents to prove Noella's culpability and that I better call her soon. He also warned me about a man named Mitch. I've been wavering on this and asking for advice."

"Well that certainly is interesting, given what Noella's just told us. There must be a person or group out to get her ... people who were either wronged by her or lost money." Richard paused then spoke once again. "I think we all need to be careful here, as the Board's reputation is at stake."

"Yes, I see your point, but I believe Noella's accusations can be equally as damaging. If we have a chance to stop her, I say we do it!" Brad said emphatically.

"I'm with you on that point Brad," said Chas. If we can hold her at bay with something that could damage her reputation, then maybe that's what it'll take."

"But are we playing the same game she is then? Are we blackmailing her right back?" asked Richard. "And what if she exposes us for blackmail in the media? What then?"

Richard seemed very concerned that Noella was such an unpredictable loose cannon, that she couldn't be trusted under any circumstances. She was hungry for power and when you combine that with money, it could be a dangerous thing.

"I'm willing to take the fall if this goes south," said Brad. "I've got to try to protect my employees and Lianna is worth putting my own ass on the line." He looked at Lianna and smiled. "I think you should call this person… Monique, is it?"

"Yes. That's right." Lianna responded. "What if we did it together in this room, and that way, everyone's on the same page. We can mute the phone if we need to consult quickly during the call."

Brad, Richard and Chas thought this was a good idea and so did Darren. "If things are getting bad, I'll just give you a signal," said Darren.

"Sounds good everyone," said Richard. "When shall we call her?"

"I say the sooner the better," said Lianna. "The caller said there's a very short window to get this information."

"How about tomorrow afternoon?" asked Brad. "I think I can be here. How about you gentlemen?" He looked up from his day timer at Chas, Richard and Darren who all agreed.

"Good," said Lianna. "I hope Monique will be available to speak to us. If not, we'll have to reschedule, but if we do, we can still talk amongst ourselves about next steps for the legal battle."

"Good idea," said Darren, who was heading the legal team for the case. "As far as your civil suit, don't worry about the date just yet. I'll take care of it all."

"Thank you so much, Darren. You don't know how much I appreciate your support here," Lianna explained. "This is all quite overwhelming."

Just then, Lianna's cell phone rang. It was her daughters' school calling and she hoped everything was ok. "Sorry gentlemen, I need to take this. We'll talk tomorrow." Lianna left the room for some privacy and then picked up the call. "Lianna Monahan speaking," she said.

"Hello Lianna, this is Bill Williams calling." It was the Principal at Dallas and Diane's school.

"Hi Bill, is everything ok?" she asked nervously.

"Well, Lianna, I'm afraid that Dallas has been in a fight here," Bill said reluctantly. "And I think I'm going to have to suspend her for a day."

Chapter 16

Lianna was shocked to hear the news and she viewed the daughter of a school principal getting suspended almost like a black mark on her own record. She had to be first and foremost concerned about Dallas and her state of mind, and she wondered what would drive her to the point of violence to solve a problem.

"Are you sure it's my Dallas, Bill?" Lianna asked, hoping there was some mistake.

"I'm afraid so, Lianna," Bill responded with an awkward chuckle but not in a disrespectful way. "We have her here at the office. Can you come meet with us for a bit this afternoon?"

"I think so," Lianna reluctantly said. "I just have to cover a class at 2:00 pm for 30 minutes, then I'll be on my way over."

"Great, we'll see you between 2:30 and 3:00 PM then," Bill replied.

"See you then, Bill." said Lianna and she ended the call, still perplexed about her daughter's behaviour and how out of character it was. She and the girls had many conversations when they were younger about using their words to solve problems and she just assumed the habits they developed then would stay with them into the teen years.

Lianna went to cover the Grade 3 class at 2:00 PM, then it was back to the office to gather her things to leave. She wouldn't be coming back to the school and spoke with Michael Kamaguchi her assistant principal about being in charge while she was gone.

"Michael, I have an urgent family matter to take care of so I need to leave. Can you please cover the office while I'm gone? I likely won't be back today."

"Of course I will," Michael replied. "Is everything ok?" he asked in a very concerned voice.

"Oh yes, no one is hurt or anything. Just something at the girls' school I need to deal with. Thanks so much, Michael. I really appreciate it."

"Anything for you, Lianna," Michael replied, being a dedicated assistant and a friend. "Take as long as you need. Everything will be fine here as long as I'm around," he stated with confidence.

"Thanks again," Lianna answered him. "Oh…and if any lawyers call for me, other than Darren Matishyn, please tell them I've quit," she said jokingly and they both laughed. She needed some comic relief at the moment and was proud of herself for trying to keep things light.

"See you tomorrow, Patricia!" Lianna said to her admin secretary, and she walked out toward her car.

When she arrived at her car, she found a flat front tire. She looked back at the other driver's side tire which was also flat, but it had been slashed with a sharp object. This was no coincidence, she thought, and she was steaming mad that someone had done this. It *had* to be intentional, as both valve caps were missing from the tires as well. The other tires fully inflated and untouched.

She knew she had to get to her daughters' school and wondered what to do. She went back into the school and down to Karen's classroom.

"Karen … sorry to interrupt, but I have a bit of an emergency. I have 2 flat tires and I need a car to get to my daughter's school. May I borrow your car for about an hour?

"No problem Lianna. Is everything ok?" asked Karen, very concerned about Lianna.

"Yes, no one is hurt, but I have to meet with the principal soon." Lianna had an urgent tone in her voice and Karen quickly got her keys out of her filing cabinet. "I hope to be back her in an hour or so Karen. Thanks so much!"

"I know you'd do the same for me Lianna. I hope everything works out."

Lianna got into Karen's car and quickly headed toward Dallas' school. Dallas had never been involved in any acts of violence in her life and that something or someone, must have really provoked her to a point of rage. Lianna continued to wonder how her daughter could be pushed to the limit and finally break.

She walked into the school and headed toward the main office, passing several students on her way in. Finally, she entered the office and saw the admin secretary.

"How can I help you?"

"I'm Lianna Monahan. I got a call from Bill Williams that my daughter Dallas is being suspended," Lianna said with hesitation.

"Oh yes. He's expecting you," said the secretary. "Just have a seat and I'll let him know you're here." Lianna felt like she herself was in trouble as she waited for the principal to arrive. Finally, she heard his footsteps.

"Ms. Monahan?" said the principal, as he reached out his hand toward

Lianna.

"Sorry I'm a few minutes late Bill. Someone just slashed the tires on my car at school." Lianna explained.

"Oh dear!" said Bill as he motioned for them to follow him into his office. "Please have a seat.".

He proceeded to explain that Dallas was in an argument with a student who made fun of Lianna. The female told Dallas that her mom was going to be fired for being a bad principal. Dallas lost it and ended up punching the student in the stomach and then pushing her to the ground. Bill said she was remorseful, but said she couldn't deal with someone insulting her mom like that. "I understand how that could really upset Dallas," said Bill, "but we never condone any actions like this to deal with a problem." Lianna understood this from a principal's perspective but was secretly proud of Dallas for standing up for her.

"So where is she now?" Lianna asked Bill.

"Just in the conference room, spending some time reflecting on her behavior," Bill responded. "Are you ready to see her?"

"How long is the suspension for?" Lianna asked.

"Well, this is her first offence, so I'm giving her one full day tomorrow," Bill said reluctantly.

"I understand," said Lianna. I will spend some time talking with her. Do you need me to bring her in when she returns to school?"

"No, it's ok." said Bill. "I'll trust that you've debriefed the incident with her. I've already spoken with both of the girls, so there's probably no need for further discussion here."

"Thank you, Bill. I'm sorry she chose to respond like this. It won't happen again, I assure you," said Lianna apologetically.

"Thanks for coming in Lianna. I'm sorry we had to meet under these circumstances. Good luck with your tires. I hope you discover who slashed them."

"Me too," said Lianna, as they got up to leave Bill's office

She picked up Dallas from the conference room and had a quiet drive back to Lianna's school. Once there, she needed to further assess what needed to be done about her car.

Lianna called the AMA, but only had one spare tire, not two. She thought that maybe they could just fill the one that wasn't slashed and she would replace the other one with a new tire this weekend.

She decided to call Todd to let him know what was going on.

"Thanks so much, Todd. Let's hope AMA can make this work," said Lianna as they spoke on the phone.

Lianna called AMA roadside assistance, and they came within 30 minutes. Todd came over from his school in case she needed a ride home.

"Is there a security camera above the parking lot?" Todd asked. He had cameras at his middle school as there was more mischief happening over there.

"As a matter of fact, we just had one installed a month ago," Lianna told him. "I'll have to go back through the footage on my computer."

"That's great," Todd responded. "I hope the camera could see who the culprits are. It would be nice to catch whoever did this."

"Absolutely!" Lianna replied. "Just hoping for a clear shot of their face so there's no guesswork."

They talked for a while and Lianna filled Todd in on her conversation with the Chief and the board's lawyer. Todd agreed that she should definitely make the call to Monique to the city offices and that Noella needed to be exposed for the kind of person she really is.

"I just hope we can find some hard evidence about Noella and that this whole thing isn't a set-up engineered by her," Lianna said with hesitation. "If it is … I'm going to be in a lot of trouble!"

Chapter 17

Lianna spoke with Dallas for a while after school, then they headed home. Dallas was remorseful, but stood by her decision to defend her mother's reputation.

"You can't imagine how mad I was," said Dallas, almost justifying her decision to hit someone.

"Oh, I can," said Lianna. "But you know I never want you to hit anyone. It's dangerous and not to mention, you could be charged by the police."

"I know Mom," Dallas replied. "I just couldn't let her get away with this. Obviously, there's some rumor out there about you and your school. Maybe your students have older brothers or sisters at my school."

"Yes, that's possible," said Lianna. "That's probably how they heard. But again, you can't go around hitting someone just because they heard a rumor."

"I get it, Mom," said Dallas. "So, what are you going to do about all this?"

"We have a plan but I can't tell you due to privacy issues," Lianna told Dallas. "It's all hush hush until we can get to court and come to a settlement."

"Well, it won't come soon enough," explained Dallas. "I know this has been hard on you, Mom."

"Yes, it has, dear," said Lianna. "We are hoping it will be over soon."

"I hope so," said Dallas sympathetically. The two of them started to make supper together and had a wonderful Mother-daughter bonding time. Diane came home just before the food was ready, and said she heard about the fight Dallas had. She was as curious about it as her mother was, but she decided not to push Dallas for details. After all, ... she was the good sister.

The next day, Lianna and the board officials were ready to call Monique at the city offices. They gathered in the conference room of the school after Lianna finished her morning routine with the students. She carefully thought about what she might say to Monique and she was a bit nervous with the others sitting in listening. She just had to know the truth about Noella and she needed to be able to discredit her character. It would not be any easy conversation as she knew Monique was risking a reputation and potentially her job to help Lianna.

"Remember," said Darren. "If you're getting into a grey area that could jeopardize the case, I will signal you like this ..." Darren held up a palm that would signal her to stop. After a minute or so, Lianna finally decided to call. She was nervous, but didn't want Monique to know it. It rang 3 times on the other end and finally a voice answered the phone. Lianna had her phone set to speaker so the others could listen. "Monique speaking," said the woman's voice.

"Hello Monique, this is Lianna Monahan calling. I got your ..."

"Oh yes Lianna," Monique interrupted. "I was expecting your call."

"I hope this is a good time to call," said Lianna.

"It's a very good time," responded Monique. "I understand that Joe called you?"

At this point, Lianna started to wonder about all the connections that

Monique might have and she became a bit nervous. Should she continue with the conversation and go to a place of safety, or should she risk violating someone's privacy and risk their jobs? She finally decided that Monique had as much to lose as she did, so she would dive right in and go for it.

"Yes, Joe called me last week and he said you have some very interesting information for me. What I have to ask is, what do you have to gain from giving it to me?" Lianna was curious to hear Monique's answer.

"Well, Lianna," Monique began, "I think you know by now what kind of person Noella is. She has proven herself over and over to be ruthless, dishonest, and hungry for power. When she was a city councilor, she made no friends and in fact, she made a lot of enemies along the way.

But she also made moves to enhance her status and gain power in the corporate world, by greasing the wheels of some companies which allowed them to get contracts they may otherwise not have gotten.

Bottom line, she decided to go to the dark side when it came to using her influence and unfortunately, I was one of the people who were manipulated by her. She threatened my livelihood if I didn't cooperate with her schemes and so I had no choice but to comply. She wasn't my boss, but … let's just say she knew things about my past that I'm not proud of and she threatened to expose me if I didn't put through the contract tenders as she requested. Is the picture becoming more clear to you, Lianna?" Monique was somewhat emotional as she continued to share her story with Lianna who felt angry and sorry for Monique as they continued to talk.

"She is just evil!" exclaimed Lianna passionately. "I can't believe she held office as long as she did. I guess she fooled a lot of people over the years and obviously took advantage of her position."

"Do you see why I want to help you, Lianna?" asked Monique.

"Absolutely, Monique. I wasn't sure whether this was a set-up engineered by Noella, but now I'm convinced that you and Joe want to help me. I understand that you can't expose Noella yourselves, but if a third party like myself gets access to documents that should be public record, then it can be done. So, what do you have for me?" Lianna asked eagerly awaiting the response.

"I have copies of city contracts with companies that Noella has been in business with," Monique carefully explained. "Her ex-husband has also dealt with them and Joe is connected with him. The ex wants to see her go down in flames, and he used Joe to make the connection with me. That is how everything fits together."

"I see," said Lianna, "so Joe is friends with Noella's ex-husband."

"Yes, that's right," responded Monique, "and Joe was mistreated by Noella as well, and not just mistreated … she threatened him."

"What did she tell him?" Lianna asked, very interested.

"At one time, Joe had an affair with Noella. Her ex knew that she was seeing someone, but he couldn't prove who it was. She threatened to expose Joe and since he was a VP in Collin De Haviland's company, she told him she'd have him fired. He was making 7 figures in salary and so he couldn't afford to lose the job, his house, and likely his wife."

"Joe was married at the time?" Lianna asked, very surprised.

"Yes, and some say Noella trapped him by seducing him at a staff party. Sources told me that she followed him into the bathroom and practically had sex with him in a stall there. Depends who you speak to but we had a reliable source. Joe's wife was also at the party but didn't find out." Monique didn't like telling this story, but she felt it was necessary to convince Lianna of Joe's experience.

"I've known what a slime she is," began Lianna, "but this is the lowest I think she's stooped to."

"I agree," said Monique, "and there are other stories of Noella's entrapment with other men she had business dealings with."

"Not surprising," said Lianna. "That just confirms what I've suspected all along.

"Did Joe mention Mitch Mason?" Monique asked.

"Yes, he did, but never told me the connection," replied Lianna. "So, when can I get the copies of these contracts?"

"Any time you want, but I need to act right away if you don't want to wait another month for them."

"Ok," said Lianna, "you can send them to me at liannam3@gmail.com. It's not my work email, and I assure you I'll keep you out of things if we get them into court. I won't ever reveal my source."

"Thank you," said Monique, "and I hope you take her down like she deserves. I'll send you the docs right after this call."

"Thank *you,*" said Lianna. "You have no idea how much you've helped us. I am so grateful to you Monique!"

"Glad to help," said Monique. "We probably shouldn't talk again

Lianna but I wish you all the best with your situation."

"Take care, Monique," said Lianna and she ended the call.

Moments later, Lianna checked her email and had 5 copies of contracts awarded by the city to various companies. At the bottom of each contract, was Monique's signature, as well as one other … the signature of Noella De Haviland.

Lianna quickly printed off the documents, and made a back-up of Monique's email. She copied the email to a flash drive, and destroyed Monique's original message.

The day went on and she spent some time in classes with kids in the afternoon, saying goodbye at the doors when they went home.

"Ms. Monahan, there's a call for you on line 2. Ms. Monahan, Line 2 please." Patricia made the announcement as Lianna was heading back to the office.

"Do you know who it is Patricia?" Lianna asked.

"It's Chief Croskenheimer," said Patricia. Lianna wondered what was going to happen next. What would be the new twist to her adventure and how would it affect what was going on in her school?

"Hi Brad," said Lianna cheerfully as she picked up the call on her office phone.

"Hello Lianna. How are you today?" the chief asked.

"Not bad Brad and you?" she replied.

"I'm doing well," said Brad, "but I just got a call from Noella's lawyer that she is now pursuing a police investigation into alleged threats she says originated from you. She said she just wants to give me a heads up before you get charged. I'm not sure what type of evidence she's ever going to come up with but she stands by her story that you sent the thugs to threaten her to back off."

Lianna was not surprised with this, after Noella burst into their last meeting. But she wondered if the people who threatened her had anything to do with the companies who were awarded the contracts with the city and if they were connected to Joe or Monique in any way.

"I have the copies of some contracts signed by Monique and Noella awarding the tenders for service to the city," said Lianna.

"Good. Can you send them to me and to Darren Matishyn in legal please? Our team has discovered some connection between Noella and some business ventures. Apparently, she has made some investments in some companies and I want to see if there's any matches with the ones Monique has found."

"I hope we can make some connections at least in one or two cases," Lianna stated. "If we can at least show her involvement, we stand a chance to discredit her and even show conflict of interest violations as a public official."

"Yes, that's what I'm hoping as well," said Brad. "We'll keep our fingers crossed for sure. How are you holding up, Lianna?" Brad was very concerned for one of his top-notch principals here and he wanted to make sure she was still ok … especially to function in her daily work.

"I'm fine Brad," Lianna explained. "I'm getting more and more of a thick skin when it comes to Noella and her tactics. Some of it seems to be empty threats and promises of action but nothing ever comes of it."

Just then, there was a knock on her door. "Just a moment Brad, I need to see who's at my door. She opened it up and a tall male with a beard and moustache pushed on the door.

"Are you Lianna Monahan?" he asked.

"Yes, I am …"

He handed her an envelope and said, "you've just been served." Then he turned around and left the office. She opened the envelope and then walked back to her phone call with Brad.

"Brad … I think I've just been served a subpoena to go to court!"

Chapter 18

"What's the document say?" asked Brad.

"It says that I am hereby required by law to attend The Court of Kings Bench in the civil case of Noella De Haviland vs. Lianna Monahan. Court date is set for July 15th. That's right in the middle of my summer! I'm on holidays! I have a trip to Europe planned and I won't even be in town!" Lianna exclaimed with a disgusted tone in her voice.

Brad chuckled slightly, then apologized. "I'm sorry Lianna, but isn't this typical for Noella to do something like that? Don't worry, Darren will ensure that he moves that hearing as well. She seems to be stacking up the lawsuits even as we speak."

"Well, she's not going to get her way on this one. I'll skip the trial if I have to…I'm going to Europe come hell or high water!" Lianna said very determined to let the chief know she'd had enough of Noella's games.

"Don't worry Lianna, she's a lightweight! Darren has handled much worse individuals in the past. That's why we still have him around," said Brad reassuringly.

Just then, Brad put Lianna on hold, and came back a moment later.

"We have now established a connection between Noella and at least two companies," Brad said enthusiastically. "We obtained a record of her investment certificates with them, both of which are dated during her time in office."

"That's good news!" exclaimed Lianna, who was so happy to hear this.

"I'm going to set up a meeting between us and Noella's lawyers to discuss this and maybe we can get her to drop the suits. Can you meet tomorrow?" Brad asked. "I don't know what time yet, but I'll let you know."

"Sounds good Brad. I'm more than ready to get this whole thing over with!" Lianna said with frustration in her voice.

"I know, Lianna. Me too. So watch your email and I'll send you a meeting request," Brad replied.

"I will Brad. Take care," Lianna said and ended the call. She now had more to worry about with the new lawsuit. It was time to go home and spend some time with her girls.

On the way to her car which was now fixed, she saw the familiar colour of Todd's car. He pulled up beside her and rolled his window down.

"So, who's ready to go for a drink?" he asked enthusiastically.

Lianna thought this sounded good especially after getting more bad news today. Lianna thought about her girls and knew they'd be ok getting something for themselves to eat.

"I'd love to, Todd. Where do you want to go?" she asked him.

"I thought maybe the Winkin' Monkey," said Todd. "I think they have fifty cent wings tonight as well. Happy hour from five to seven."

"Sounds great!" Lianna replied. "I'll follow you there."

Todd pulled out of the parking lot and Lianna soon followed him. As she drove, she checked her rear-view mirror as she always did and noticed that a familiar blue car was following her. She'd seen it before and as she made several turns, the car stayed with her. She decided to drive faster and take a few more unnecessary turns to confirm her suspicions. Sure enough, the car kept following.

She noticed a police car parked along the curb ahead, and seeing an officer in the driver's seat, she suddenly pulled up beside it and stopped. The car behind her had to make a quick stop and Lianna rolled her window down and motioned to the officer.

"I need your help. The car behind me has followed me aggressively for the past 10 minutes and I think I'm in danger," she exclaimed frantically.

Suddenly, the car behind her reversed, then went speeding past her. Lianna had the police cruiser blocked however and by the time she moved away to let them out, the car had sped off and was nowhere to be seen.

The officer pulled up behind her and turned on his lights. "I'm sorry miss. I tried to get out quickly but the car was too fast. Are you ok?" he asked her.

"Yes, but I'm sure they were following me to intimidate or even worse, cause me harm. What can you do with a license plate number?" Lianna asked.

"I can file a report," the officer explained, "but you'll have to come to the station. We can't pursue anyone without just cause, and we'll need to assess the immediate danger you're experiencing. I'm sorry...it's just procedure miss."

"I understand you have rules, but would you have followed the car if I hadn't been in the way now?" Lianna asked, hoping for a positive response.

"Actually, I wouldn't have been able to Miss. My job was to ensure your immediate safety, so I had to stop and check on you first," the officer explained with empathy.

"Ok ... I understand that part," said Lianna. "So, what I'm hearing is you'd have to witness a direct threat in this situation before you'd pursue a suspect?"

"Yes, that's pretty much how it works," the officer explained reluctantly.

"Do you have a blank report form I can take with me and bring into the station later?" Lianna asked.

She was frustrated but she understood what the police role was here. She decided she would file the report later, and wanted to keep her drink date with Todd. She thanked the officer and was on her way.

She entered the Winkin' Monkey, a neighborhood bar not far from Todd's school. It was dark at first and as her eyes adjusted to the change in lighting, she looked at the walls which were filled with memorabilia from years past. There was something of interest for everyone, from sports enthusiasts, to rodeo cowboys, to eclectic antiques which also included 100-year-old photos of the city and its early beginnings. She also saw beautiful tapestries of a multitude of colours on the wall representing different cultural groups from around the world as well as pride flags, showing support for the LGBTQ community. In all, it was an incredible visual experience with so many symbols depicting modern life.

She spotted Todd in the corner who was waving her over and smiling.

She couldn't wait to tell him about the vehicle that followed her and get his advice about what to do next. Lianna was fearful for her life now, and Todd was a beacon in the storm of all that was going on.

"I'm so glad to see you, Lianna. I thought maybe you changed your mind," Todd said with a hint of relief in his voice.

"It almost did," Lianna said with a concerned voice.

"Oh my God! Really?" Todd said, sounding very worried. "What happened? I also started to worry that you might have been in an accident or something."

"Awe ... thanks Todd. I'm OK. I was followed for a while after I left the parking lot though."

"What?" Todd said with alarm. "What happened?" Todd looked at her and she knew he cared so much for her that it shook him up a bit.

"I noticed a blue car in my rearview mirror and I kept looking back and it was always there. I decided to do some 'evasive' driving to see if it really was following me and sure enough it was. I sped up, making multiple turns, but after each turn, the car was still behind me. It got closer and closer and so I finally spotted a police cruiser parked on the side of the road. I pulled up beside it and stopped abruptly and the car behind had to slam on their brakes. As I put down the window to talk to the officer, the car reversed and sped off. I was really scared!" Lianna relived the moments in her mind and became even more anxious.

"Oh my God, Lianna! Are you ok now?" Todd asked with great concern. He didn't like the fact that she was shaken up by this incident. "What did the officer do for you?"

"I've calmed down now," she said. "I have a blank report form to fill in and take to the station later. I need to do it while everything is fresh in my memory."

"I'm so relieved you're ok," said Todd. "Do you think it might have been Noella's people?"

"Without a doubt," Lianna replied. "She's taken this thing to a new level and I'm really worried Todd," Lianna exclaimed.

"You know I'm here for you, Lianna." Todd reassured her. "I won't let anything happen to you, my love!"

"You're amazing, Todd, and I know you really mean it. But how can you be with me all the time? You can't … it's just not possible," Lianna explained.

"I know," said Todd. "But as long as I'm around, I won't let anyone hurt you."

Lianna felt tears coming into her eyes. She hadn't felt these feelings for a man since her divorce and she was feeling fortunate that Todd was still around in spite of all the turmoil. She knew he loved her and this was so comforting to her. He was everything a woman could want in a man. She reached out her hand and she took it in his own, caressing it gently.

Todd gazed into her eyes and she felt a sense of calmness that she only felt when he looked at her. She was so lucky to have this man in her life right now and there was nothing she wanted more than to have his love.

They sat together for the next hour, Todd reassuring her of her safety and Lianna responding to his care and concern. They talked about Noella for a bit and the current state of the lawsuits. She asked for Todd's advice and how to cope with what was going on. She told him about the documents Monique sent to her and he supported her decision to share these with the legal team.

"We have to put pressure on her or nothing's going to change," said Lianna. "I have to get tough now and very quickly apply pressure or she's going to eat me up in court."

"I agree Lianna and I'm 100 percent behind you. You will always have my support and I'm here if I can do anything for you," said Todd.

"Let me get the bill today, Todd," offered Lianna kindly. "I think it must be my turn by now, isn't it?"

"I don't keep track of that sort of thing Lianna, but I'd love it if you bought the drinks today," Todd said humbly.

"Then it's settled … I'm paying!" Lianna exclaimed with a satisfied tone of voice. She motioned for the server to bring the bill to the table and she soon paid and they were on their way.

"What am I going to do if I see that car again?" Lianna asked Todd with a worried tone in her voice. "Should I call the police?"

"I think so," answered Todd. "I know they seem to want to catch the perps in the act, but you need to feel safe. I'd call 911 if they are following you."

"Ok. I think you're right Todd, and I will. Right now, I need to get that report done and take it to the police station. Will you follow me home and maybe come in for a bit?" Lianna asked hoping Todd would oblige.

"Of course I will," Todd replied and he was happy to help her feel safer.

They drove to Lianna's condo and both cars went down into the underground parking garage. When she arrived at her parking stall, she noticed an unusual colour on the pavement of her stall and was shocked at the spray-painted message she saw.

Chapter 19

Todd parked his car, and came over to Lianna's stall, noticing she had not yet pulled in. When he read the words on the ground, anger came to his face, as he was visibly upset. He knew Lianna was so incensed by what she saw, and that she now felt far worse than she had before. How would she respond?

"I can't believe someone could write this!" exclaimed Lianna with anger in her voice.

"Me neither," added Todd as they both looked in disbelief. The stall had a base colour of red, with images of a skull in each corner. In the center was written the words *Principal Child Killer!* This was extremely upsetting to both of them as nothing could have been further from the truth. Todd came over and hugged Lianna as she broke down in tears, shaking her head and repeating the word 'NO!' over and over again. Someone who dedicated herself to children in both her personal and professional life should never be subjected to this extreme kind of hate. Lianna was now determined to take Noella down no matter how she did it.

She called the police who decided to take this as a threat to her safety and they said they would contact her in the next few days. In the meantime, her condo maintenance people cleaned the vandalized stall as much as they could and repainted it grey.

Lianna was thankful for this but she was still very bothered by the message and the bold and brazen approach of her enemy. Was it Noella or was it some other sinister group of people who wanted her gone?

****

It was Tuesday and the next School Board meeting was in a few hours. Lianna knew that there would be an *in-camera* meeting beforehand, and she was invited to join them as a guest to talk about Noella and her situation.

Lianna wrapped things up at school, and headed home to try catching her girls before heading to the meeting. She got into her car and drove away from the school. She kept checking her rearview mirror for the car that followed her before, but didn't see any sign of a vehicle tracking her.

She arrived at home, walked through the lobby saying hi to Alfred, and continued up the elevator to her floor. As she walked off the elevator, she heard voices down the hall toward her unit. As she approached, she saw police officers in uniform as well as in plain clothes and her condo door was open. She ran toward the door and was stopped by a female officer who asked who she was.

"I'm Lianna Monahan and this is my place! Where are my girls?" she asked frantically.

"There's no one here Ms. Monahan, but it appears that someone has broken into your condo," said the officer. "There was no one inside when we arrived. One of your neighbors heard banging sounds and called the concierge who then called the police."

"Can I go inside?" Lianna asked. "Have you seen two teenage girls around?"

"I'm afraid not," the officer said. "CSI team is still looking for evidence and we haven't seen any kids here." Lianna was both worried and relieved at the same time.

"When can I go in?" Lianna asked. "I need to check on a few things."

She seemed very distraught and was worried that whoever broke in might have discovered Moniques contracts.

"We'll need another hour or so to dust for prints and so on. Shouldn't be much longer than that," said the officer. Lianna decided to call Diane's cell phone and see where the girls were.

"Diane ... it's Mom. Where are you and Dallas?"

"I've just left the school, but I don't know where Dallas is. I haven't talked to her since this morning," Diane explained. Lianna was a bit worried but didn't want Diane to be shocked when she arrived home.

"Diane, our place was broken into today," said Lianna.

"*WHAT!*" said Diane very surprised and upset.

"The police are conducting their investigation right now, and I can't get in our place for another hour or so. You can come home if you want or wait an hour ... it's up to you." Lianna stayed calm as she explained the situation to Diane.

"No mom ... I'll come home and we can wait together," Diane said and she ended the call with Lianna. Diane was quite calm about things during times of crisis, and Lianna was very proud of the way her daughter was able to regulate her emotions in spite of the trauma of the divorce.

"Ms. Monahan, can you think of anyone that would want to break into your place?" asked the officer. Lianna badly wanted to implicate Noella but she stopped short of giving the police her name.

"I am being sued right now for negligence at my school but other than that, I can't think of anyone who'd want to break in," said Lianna. "We live a very basic and simple life here."

"You said you have daughters, correct?" said the officer.

"Right. Two daughters 14 and 16 years old," replied Lianna.

"Have either of them had disagreements with anyone lately?" the officer probed. Lianna didn't want to lie so she told her about the fight Dallas had been in at school.

"Well, I really doubt that the break-in is related to that, Ms. Monahan, but we'll keep it in mind. Thanks for your time and I'll be in touch if we find anything."

Lianna decided to go down and talk with Alfred about the break in to see if he saw or talked with anyone going up the elevator. She arrived in the lobby just as an officer was wrapping up a conversation with Alfred.

"Ms. Monahan, I'm so sorry to hear about your place. I feel so bad that someone was able to go up the elevator without me knowing," said Alfred. "You know I keep a good watch all the time."

"I know, Alfred," Lianna said understandingly, "I don't blame you at all. Did you see anyone unusual or different than the tenants? Any service or repair people maybe?"

"Now that you mention it, there was a repair person with Telemark Internet. He showed me a work order for a unit on your floor. I assumed he was legit. He had a name tag with photo ID and everything." Alfred felt bad about this but he did his due diligence in checking the repair person's ID.

"It's OK Alfred. It's not your fault. You have to be able to let people in," said Lianna. I'm not upset with you. Please know that."

"I feel like I am sort of responsible, Miss," he said.

"Don't even give it another thought," Lianna replied. She gave him a hug and then she saw Diane coming up the front walk to the condo doors. "Here's one of my dear daughters now."

Diane didn't say anything but came straight toward Lianna and gave her a hug. Lianna had to hold back the tears and decided to put on a brave face for her. She could tell Diane was very upset, but trying to stay calm. Like Mother … like daughter she thought.

Lianna opened her purse and took a look to see if the flash drive was still there. She was relieved to see it was, as she had destroyed the paper copies of the contracts.

"So, what now?" asked Diane. "Do we move or do we stay put and wonder if someone will come back?"

"We'll have to talk about all that," said Lianna. "In the meantime, how was your day?"

"Pretty good Mom. Just a couple of exams, but I don't get phased by those. It's just part of school. I just wish the teachers were a little more enthusiastic sometimes."

Diane was a realist, and a good student who had high expectations for teachers though. "Oh … I just remembered that Dallas has practice after school today. I think she said she'll be home by 5:00 pm."

"That's good. I was hoping we could have a quick supper together, but now I'm not sure if we can cook," Lianna stated.

"Looks like we're skipping the dishes tonight!" joked Diane as she laughed with her mother. The two of them headed toward the elevator and took it up to their floor. As they approached the unit, a plain clothes detective stopped them to ask a question or two.

"I'll do my best to answer," said Lianna, but I'm really burnt out right now and so is my daughter. Anything we can help with is important to us but just realize we're very tired."

"I understand, Ms. Monahan. Do you have any names for us ... you know, of the people from the lawsuit?" the detective asked.

Lianna thought carefully before answering as she wasn't sure how implicating Noella would be helpful at this time. With the pending legal battle, she wondered if it might affect the process in the upcoming trial.

"I can't tell you specifically at this point," said Lianna. "I believe there is a group of people who feel I haven't done my due diligence in keeping the students safe in my school building. We always have some vocal parents and that just goes with the job."

"I see," responded the detective, "well I guess we will do our best to track down the culprits who did this. You can go back in your condo now, and let us know if you think of anything."

"Thank you, detective. We will," Lianna replied.

Lianna and Diane entered their apartment and felt an awful sensation ... they felt violated and neither of them wanted to look around to see the aftermath. Drawers were left open, clothing spread about all over the floor and papers were obviously rifled through in several areas.

Fortunately, nothing was vandalized or damaged, but it was obvious that the offenders were searching for something. Lianna knew what that was, but she hadn't told the girls about the documents Monique had sent. She thought if she did, the girls would blame her for the break in.

"OMG! I can't believe the mess they left behind, Mom," said Diane in a disgusted tone of voice. "My room was ripped apart. My laptop is gone and my tablet. Do you think they were after some information?"

"It's possible," said Lianna, not wanting to lie to Diane but not revealing anything about the documents. "Is anything else of yours missing?"

"Doesn't seem to be," said Diane. "I'll keep checking my stuff."

Just then, Dallas walked through the door and couldn't believe her eyes. She rushed to her room to see if anything had happened there and returned looking very mad.

"WTF Mom!" Dallas exclaimed. "What happened here?"

"We've had a break in, Dallas," Lianna said calmly. "It happened while we were gone today."

"Why us? We don't have much to steal," Dallas said. "What could they possibly want in our house?"

Lianna was starting to feel guilty about the contracts from Monique, but how would Noella know that she had them? Did Noella have some way of monitoring what Monique was sending to her? She thought she better fill the girls in on what was going on.

"Ok girls, there's something I need to tell you." Lianna began. "Let's sit down at the table and I'll explain it all."

She and the girls sat in the dining room and Lianna explained all that had transpired with the phone call from Joe and her conversation with Monique. She told the girls that this was highly confidential but that it was going to help in the school board's battle with Noella.

"So, they must have been looking for the flash drive, which I carried with me in my purse," explained Lianna. "I'm so sorry, I never thought anyone would know that Monique sent me the documents." Lianna felt bad but was glad she came clean with her daughters and told them what was going on.

"It's ok Mom," said Diane. "We just want this whole thing over with … for your sake."

"Thank you, Diane. I appreciate your understanding, and I hope there'll be no more trouble," Lianna told her daughter sympathetically.

"Can we call skip the dishes now, please?" asked Dallas. "I'm starving after practice."

"Are you girls ok with pizza?" asked Lianna.

"For sure, Mom," answered Diane, and Dallas nodded her head as well.

Lianna picked up her cell phone and ordered Domino's Pizza which would be delivered in 15 minutes. Lianna had to go to the meeting in about 1 hour, so they'd be able to eat supper together before she left. They sat and talked and soon there was a knock at the door.

"Pizza must be here!" Dallas said excitedly, and she ran to the door to get it. When she opened the door, she was shocked to see who was standing in the hallway. It couldn't be!

Chapter 20

"Daddy! What are you doing here?" Dallas asked, both excited and nervous at the same time.

"Can I come in?" her father asked. Dallas looked back at her mother who gave her a nod and moved toward the door to greet her ex-husband.

"Dave. To what do we owe this unannounced visit?" Lianna asked with some hesitation and annoyance in her voice.

"Well, I heard there was some trouble here at the condo and thought I'd drop in and make sure you were all ok," he responded sounding sincerely concerned. Lianna didn't like him just dropping in without calling first. Lianna and Dave split up with a very messy divorce and she still harbored much ill will toward him. Diane was a little less accepting of her father's faults than Dallas, and Dallas was always happy to spend time with him, no matter how short it was.

"So how did you hear about our trouble so quickly," Lianna asked, very suspicious of his motives and how he got the information. She wondered who his source was and that was also very concerning to her.

"A little birdie told me," joked Dave, hoping to distract Lianna from the question at hand. "By the way, did you get the payment from me this month?" he quickly interjected.

"Yes, I did," Lianna said, "but you still didn't answer my question." She looked at Dave and he just smiled.

"Hey Pumpkin," Dave said turning back to Dallas, "would you and your sister like to go camping in the mountains this weekend?" he asked again, attempting to distract Lianna.

"Sounds great, Dad. But I have a game Friday night. We can go Saturday morning though," said Dallas.

"How about you, Diane," he asked and he smiled at his eldest daughter hoping she would go.

"We'll see, Dad. I've got a ton of assignments due Monday so I'll have to see what I can get done this week." Lianna still didn't have an answer to her question but she decided to let it go. At least he was concerned enough to drop by, and she appreciated his concern for the girls.

"So, what was stolen from here?" Dave asked. "Electronics I bet."

"Well Diane had her computer and her tablet stolen, I'm not sure about Dallas at this point," Lianna stated. "I haven't been through my room yet, but I know there wasn't much of value except for the wedding ring."

"What!" said Dave. "You haven't sold that at the pawn shop yet?" He had a smile on his face that said he was teasing but Lianna knew he wouldn't have been surprised if she sold it.

Dave wandered through the condo looking at the after-effects of the break in and shaking his head. "I feel so bad for you guys," he said as he examined the chaos. "Do you want help cleaning this up?"

"I think we're good," said Lianna. "Besides, we were about to have supper, then I have a meeting to get to."

Dave looked at the oven and the counter tops and saw no evidence of food preparation. In his haste, he said, "Ahhh…Mom's cooking again!" And at that moment, there was another knock at the door. "Must be Skip the Cooking arriving with your dinner," he said sarcastically and smiled at Dallas who didn't smile back at him. He got cold looks from all three of the girls and took this as a sign that maybe he outstayed his welcome.

"I better get going," he said. "But if you need any help, let me know and I'll be here."

Lianna went to answer the door and received the food they ordered. She then took the opportunity to get a shot in at Dave. "Look Dave, it's the trainer for your next career," as she pointed to the delivery driver. "No offence, by the way. You're great at delivery," she said to the driver. "I just hope Dave can be half as good as you are after 10 years!"

Dave laughed and then he said, "Touché Lianna!" and then he headed out the door. Lianna and the girls enjoyed a quiet dinner of pizza, before Lianna got ready to leave for the Board meeting.

"I'm sorry girls, but the chief needs to see me before the big meeting tonight," she apologized to the girls.

"We understand, Mom, and if it's going to get us over this whole thing faster, then we support you," said Dallas.

"Thank you, sweetheart" replied Lianna as she grabbed her purse and work bag. "I should hopefully be home around 10:00 P.M. but in case I'm not, make sure you get some rest tonight."

"We will, Mom," replied Diane. "Good luck tonight …and don't take any crap from anyone!" she added.

Lianna headed out the door, and as she approached the elevator, she noticed a man just standing a few meters away down the hall. He had on a black hoodie, black pants, and sunglasses, so she couldn't see his face well. Lianna was concerned. She immediately got on her phone and called the police non-emergency number as she got closer to the elevator.

"Is this the police non-emergency number?" she asked.

"It is miss. ... Could you hold on just a moment please?" She pushed the button to get the elevator down and out of the corner of her eye, she saw the man turn and head toward the stairwell exit. He disappeared into the stairwell and soon the elevator came. She pushed the button to select the parking garage, but was unsure about going in there alone.

"I think someone is following me. I'm at 1642 Belaire Crescent at Davenport Place. What's that? ... yes, I'm alone but I have you on the phone obviously...no I haven't seen him before but I ... yes, I'm in an elevator heading to the parking garage... ok. I'll keep you on the phone while I go to my car...thank you!"

Lianna got off the elevator and headed to her car. As she approached, she saw someone at the end of the garage who had black pants and a hoodie. It was the man from her floor.

"I see him watching me from the end of the garage ... yes I'm sure ...he's ..." Lianna turned briefly toward her car, looked again and this time saw no one. Was she hallucinating? Did she just imagine the whole thing?

Suddenly, she felt a hand on her shoulder! She screamed and spun around into a defensive position, quickly reaching into her bag for pepper spray. Much to her surprise, it was Todd!

"Oh my God, Todd! You scared the crap out of me! I've just been followed by a man in black pants and a hoodie… he was right … there!" Lianna said with fear in her voice. "When you touched my shoulder I … well never mind."

"Are you ok, mam?" asked the officer on the phone. Lianna suddenly remembered she was on the phone with police and responded, "Yes, I'm with a friend now. Thank you!"

"I'm so sorry!" said Todd. "I was just coming to see if you wanted some company at the Board meeting tonight. I have some interest in something on the board's agenda tonight … besides your case. You're important but … oh I'm messing this up, aren't I?" Todd said feeling embarrassed.

"It's OK Todd. I get it and yes, I'd love some company tonight." Lianna said with relief in her voice. "Can we take your car, then you can drop me off after? I'm so freaked out here Todd. Now I'm worried about my girls too!" Lianna was almost starting to hyperventilate.

"It's going to be OK, Lianna. Let's take a deep breath together … ready … breathe in … 1, 2, 3 ,4 ,5 … and out … 1, 2, 3, 4, 5 … that's it… and again …" Todd led her through a couple rounds of breathing techniques until she finally looked calm.

"Thank you, Todd…I needed that. Things are just so crazy right now. Can you stay with me tonight …please?" said Lianna almost in a tone of desperation.

"I think so," said Todd. "I just have to check with my boys on a couple things. You have a meeting *before* the board meeting, correct?"

"Yes, my meeting is at 6:15. Board meeting starts at 7:00," said Lianna. She got into Todd's car, and together they headed to the Board offices. She had never remembered a time when she was this stressed about work and now it was also a fear for her personal safety.

It was almost more than she could handle, but she kept telling herself *I'm a strong independent woman and I can do this*. Lianna kept trying to breathe and engage in her own relaxation activity as they drove.

They arrived at the parking lot around 6:05 and Todd found a spot close to the entrance. To make sure Lianna felt safe, he walked with her all the way to the building. Once inside, Lianna found her way to the conference room beside the board council chamber.

"I have to take it from here, Todd, but I'll see you in the chamber for the main meeting," Lianna said with some reservation as she was nervous about what might happen next.

"I'll be close so don't you worry, sweetheart," Todd reassured her. Remember I'm not going to let anything happen to you."

"Thank you, Todd. I don't know what I'd do without you right now," Lianna confided in him. "I'll see you after my in-camera meeting."

Lianna turned and walked into the conference room while Todd sat down on a bench in the hallway. He knew she needed his support and was determined to stay close. Soon it was 6:15 and the conference room door closed.

"Hello, Lianna. Good to see you again," said Chas, chair of the elected school board.

"You of course know Brad as well as our Legal counsel Darren Matishyn. This is Madeline Moriarty, our communications specialist and Stacey Lindholm the head of our HR department."

Lianna was wondering why Madeline and Stacey were there and was a bit nervous.

"Nice to meet you, Madeline," Lianna said as she shook her hand. She likewise did the same with Stacey and then they all sat down to get started.

"So, Lianna, the Board has taken a close look at the situation with Noella," Chas began to explain. "We have considered all angles from an HR perspective as well as public relations one and after careful consideration, we feel it might be best for you to take a leave for a short time until some of the dust blows over. We know you're doing a great job, but we're also worried about you and your family's safety. I understand you've had some close calls with dangerous situations lately?"

"Yes," said Lianna. "I'd be lying if I said I hadn't and I'd be fooling everyone if I said I wasn't afraid for my safety…and my kids." Lianna understood why they might want her to go on leave, but she really wanted to stay strong and not show any weakness when it came to Noella and the lawsuits.

"So how do you feel about taking a leave right now?" asked Stacey. Lianna was silent for a moment and then spoke.

"Honestly, I'd prefer not to, but I understand your perspective, and the need to maintain a positive image for the board," said Lianna.

"If you publicize my leave however, I wouldn't agree to that as the media will have a hay day with it and I'll look guilty. So, if you need me to go on leave, I will but I want it to be a private matter. I'd also like some input about who will be in charge of my school when I'm gone."

"I think we can accommodate those things Lianna," said Chas. "How soon are you willing to start the leave?"

"Well, I just need a few days to get some things in order at the school and of course, I want to spend some time with my replacement," Lianna said confidently.

"No problem," said Chas. "We can give it a week or so."

Lianna had mixed feelings about the leave, but she understood. The meeting ended and Lianna went to find Todd. She walked down the long hallway toward the meeting chamber but couldn't see Todd. When she walked inside the meeting chamber who should she see but Noella De Haviland.

She finally saw Todd on the other side of the chamber so she walked over and sat with him in the gallery. She explained to Todd about the upcoming leave and he consoled her as best he could. Noella was glaring at both of them and Lianna chose to look away and ignore her. How did Noella know she'd be there and what was she up to now?

Chapter 21

Lianna was worried about how she'd feel while off work, and how the students would be told about her leave. She arrived at Carlton the next morning feeling a bit melancholy but realizing she was doing the right thing for the school and the community. After a few minutes in her office, teacher Jason Regere dropped by to say hello.

"Good morning, Lianna," he said cheerfully. "How are things?" Jason was unaware of what had transpired the night before.

"Not bad, Jason, but I'm calling a stand-up meeting before the kids come in today. I have some things to share." Lianna looked at him and he knew something wasn't right.

"Are you ok, Lianna?" Jason asked with a concerned tone. "You look worried for some reason … no offence by the way."

"Actually, Jason, I'm a bit sad today, and I'll explain it all at the meeting. Thanks for your concern. I appreciate it," Lianna responded, and Jason decided to let her be.

He was worried about her as she was always so positive with all the staff. Jason then went to his mailbox, then off to his classroom. Patricia arrived soon after and said good morning to Lianna. Lianna greeted her and she immediately knew something was wrong. Patricia was the one who knew Lianna the best, and there was no hiding feelings from the experienced support staff who stood by Lianna's side through thick and thin.

"Ok," said Patricia. "What's wrong?" She was always straight up with Lianna who couldn't bring herself to say she was fine when she wasn't.

"I'm upset today, Patricia," said Lianna sadly. "I have to call a meeting before school to let the staff know I'm going on leave. Lianna looked into Patricia's eyes that were welling up with tears.

"This is about Noella isn't it," Patricia said with almost an angry tone in her voice. Patricia would defend Lianna to the end of the earth and she knew Lianna was being mistreated by Noella. "It's not fair that you're the one who needs to adjust your life to accommodate her," added Patricia. "I am *so* upset for you I can't put it into words!" Patricia came over and gave Lianna a huge hug. Lianna appreciated the heartfelt affection Patricia was showing her and held on for a moment longer.

"Thank you, Patricia," said Lianna. "You don't know how much I needed your hug right now."

"Oh, but I do know, Ms. Lianna." said Patricia with a knowing look. "I'm a mother and a grandma remember!" and she smiled at Lianna with a warm and loving look. "What time do you want to bring the staff together?"

"I think 7:55 before the first staff go out on supervision," Lianna replied. Most of the staff were usually in the building by that time, so Lianna knew the meeting would be well attended.

She returned to her office and saw she had a voicemail on her school phone, so she listened to the message. It was Brad calling telling her that they'd found a temporary administrative sub to perform her duties while she was away.

Tony Barrenger would arrive this afternoon and spend time with Lianna the next two days. She would begin her leave at the end of the day on Friday.

Again, she felt like she was being set aside, but it was for the good of the school and the system.

"Can we please get all available staff to the staffroom for an important update," Patricia announced over the PA system. Lianna was the first one to get down the hall to the room where she would announce her leave. She poured herself a coffee and made it extra sweet this time, to add some comfort to the day. Normally she put it one spoon of sugar, but it was shaping up to be a two-spoon day.

"Ok," announced the first staff member Shannon Delco who was a great leader and a positive person on the staff. "What is so important that you needed to interrupt my morning online yoga class?" she joked with Lianna who appreciated the humor right about now. When Shannon looked at Lianna, she knew something wasn't right and she said, "oops, bad timing?"

"It's quite alright," said Lianna. "I'm welcoming comic relief today."

"Is it bad news?" asked Shannon, who was now very concerned.

"It's not great," replied Lianna, who was trying not to get too emotional. She looked away momentarily to regain composure.

"It's that bitch again isn't it!" said Shannon with anger in her voice. She knew she shouldn't call parents names, but she also knew how much Lianna had been affected by Noella's treatment. "That was my inside voice and I'm sorry for being out of line," Shannon added right away.

"It's ok, really," said Lianna who secretly shared the sentiment. "I'll just give people another minute before I start." One by one, the staff filed in, many in good spirits, but some very tired from the start of the week. There was both laughter as well as silence as everyone was wondering what the update was about.

"Thank you for coming my friends," said Lianna, as she began the difficult speech to her team.

"As you know, I've been going through a rough time with one of our parents who is now after my job. To be honest, she's accusing me of providing an unsafe environment for kids due to a couple reports she saw from the maintenance department about asbestos in our building." Lianna had to pause to regain her composure.

"Now as you know, the board always takes measures to ensure that no asbestos is exposed, but due to the age of schools in our city, they still contain a lot of materials that were used in construction before asbestos was banned."

The staff looked sympathetically at Lianna, who was having trouble keeping back the tears.

"I am named in two lawsuits right now, and I'm the target of one specifically due to comments I made about a parent. I met with school board executives, as well as our chief superintendent and their lawyer and they have decided it is in my best interest, and the Board's, for me to take a leave of absence until things have settled down.

So … as of the end of the day Friday, you will have a substitute principal in my place. Michael will provide guidance for day-to-day operations, but basically the admin sub will be ultimately responsible in my absence. The sub for me is Tony Barrenger and he will join us tomorrow." Lianna was matter of fact in informing the staff of her leave, but she had a lump in her throat while speaking. Everyone looked stunned and were quiet after she stopped talking.

"What can we do to help?" asked Mary McKinley, a veteran Grade 1 teacher.

"The only thing you can do Mary, is to continue to be the very best teachers I know you all are, and ensure the students that I'll be back in a while. They'll probably ask how long, and I'm afraid you'll just have to say that Ms. Monahan's "boss" will decide that. Please reassure them that I'm not dying or in any trouble, and that I can't wait to come back to see them. Tell them I'll miss them and please reassure them that things are going to be ok." Lianna then started to cry and several of the staff got up and came over to her to give her hugs. Some of the teachers began to cry and Lianna said, "Oh! Stop that!" as she tried to chuckle a bit to make herself feel better.

The supervision bell rang and it was time for some teachers to go outside with students. "Let's try to make this a great day everyone!" Lianna exclaimed.

Just then, Patricia came in and let Lianna know that Todd was on line one. She immediately went to her office, closed the door and picked up the phone.

"You have perfect timing Todd. How is it you know exactly when I need you the most?" Lianna said with gratitude in her voice.

"I guess I must be psychic," said Todd boastfully, but with compassion at the same time. "I'm guessing you met with the staff?" he added.

"Yes, and it was tough," Lianna explained. "They were supportive though, but it's going to be hard to give up my position to a temporary administrator. My Assistant Michael, will do well and will guide the daily operations as he knows the school the best."

"I know it will be hard on you sweetheart, but I am here for you ... 100 percent!" Todd reassured her. They spoke for another 5 minutes, then agreed to meet for a drink after work.

Lianna closed herself into her office and asked not to be disturbed and while she was there, Michael would look after all concerns and issues in the school. As an experienced Assistant Principal ... he was very good at it.

Lianna prepared all the necessary things to help Tony Barringer look after the school and organized her office with every important document and file at the ready. She had one folder that she called her "hit by a bus" folder, and if she walked out the door and *was* hit by a bus ... someone could come in and run the school in her place. In other words, she was replaceable on a moment's notice.

As the bell rang at the end of the day, she said goodbye to the children at the doors then made her way back to the office.

Much to her displeasure she arrived to find Noella sitting on a chair in her office, with an open file in front of her. Lianna checked to see if it was one of her own and in fact ... it was.

"Excuse me Ms. De Havilland, I believe that file belongs to me and has confidential information that you aren't privy to." Lianna was quite upset but kept her cool. She reached for the folder, and when Noella didn't respond, she grabbed it from her.

"Now, now, Ms. Monahan," Noella began, "aren't we getting a little rude with your number one parent? Especially one who has your career in her hands?"

Lianna thought for a moment and then chose not to engage in an argument. "What do you want, Noella?" Lianna asked with an impatient tone in her voice.

"Other than your job," began Noella, "I came to see if you've talked to the maintenance department lately." Noella seemed to know something Lianna didn't.

"Can't say that I have Ms. De Havilland. Is there something I need to know?" Lianna responded. She was fed up with Noella's games and this was one more attempt to waste her time.

"Well …" Noella began with a pretentious tone, "If you paid attention, maybe you'd know about the inspection of the building tomorrow."

I thought maybe if I told you, you'd run around like a crazy woman trying to hide exposed asbestos or something."

"Why would I do that?" asked Lianna. "There are no problems or violations."

"Are you *really* sure about that?" asked Noella, as if she knew there were problems. This was all part of her mind games and threats she liked to play with Lianna, and Lianna wasn't going to engage now.

"100 percent!" exclaimed Lianna, as she stood above Noella who was still in a chair by the door.

Lianna had to decide how to get Noella to leave, and wasn't quite sure how to do that. She finally decided to tell Noella she had a meeting in another part of the school.

"I'm afraid you need to leave now," said Lianna. "I have a meeting with some teachers." Lianna moved and pointed toward the door. Noella sat still for a moment and finally spoke again.

"If I were you ... and thank god I'm not," said Noella, "I'd be checking my building for violations. You never know when there might be a change since the previous reports. If you're not sure, try talking to Mitch."

"I'll take that under advisement," said Lianna sarcastically and she motioned to the door once again. Noella flipped her hair back, took out a make-up mirror, checked her face and then proceeded to the door.

"By the way Ms. Monahan," Noella began, "I hear you've been suspended indefinitely. At least that's what my sources tell me, and I have some pretty reliable sources!" Noella was almost out the door when she turned to face Lianna once again.

"You know you won't be back here, don't you?" Noella said with an evil grin on her face. She glared at Lianna in a threatening way, began to laugh in an almost evil tone as she headed toward the main office exit.

Lianna felt shaken by the conversation but not defeated. She'd document this behaviour and talk to Todd when they met for drinks. Tomorrow, she would meet her replacement ... and she was not enthused.

Chapter 22

Lianna left the school shortly after, and went to meet Todd at the lounge. While she drove, she talked to herself about the conversation with Noella and the more she thought about it, the more she knew Noella was playing more mind games. What did Mitch know that she didn't? Would safety inspectors from the government really be coming tomorrow? She could not be sure, but usually they would let schools know.

She found a good parking spot, then hurried into the bar where Todd had been waiting. He stood up as she entered and greeted her with a big hug.

"Did you get delayed?" he asked politely, as she seemed a little flustered.

"Guess who dropped by my office unannounced?" Lianna said to Todd. She looked frustrated and Todd could tell he needed to tread lightly as he answered.

"I'm going to say your arch nemesis, Noella Deville," Todd said, hoping she would catch the humor in his new nick name for Noella. He chuckled lightly then looked at her for a reaction.

"That's a good name for her, Todd!" Lianna said with approval, as they both laughed together. Todd knew how to take a bad situation and make it better with humor and she always appreciated that.

"I will be happy when I don't have to see her evil face anymore," Lianna explained, and she sat down and grabbed the drink menu. "Let's see … do they serve hemlock here?" she jokingly asked. Todd smiled and then responded.

"No but I think they have arsenic at happy hour prices!" Todd said as he continued the banter. He was determined to cheer her up as they both decided on their drinks.

Soon, a server came over and asked if they were ready to order and they both decided on a good IPA beer. It was a favorite of Todd's and Lianna had recently acquired a taste for a more "hoppy" drink.

Soon they were deep in conversation about Lianna's leave and the things she might need to do to help Tony. Todd reassured her that the temporaries were usually retired principals with lots of experience and that she needn't worry.

"I just feel like I need to do more before I turn things over to him," said Lianna with a worried tone. "It's my life we're talking about here and someone could screw it up within minutes!" she stated with concern.

"Remember you need to separate your career from who you are. You aren't your job and the job isn't you," Todd said in a philosophical way, hoping Lianna would see his point.

"I know," she replied, "but I just can't get past not being in control right now." Lianna looked even more worried and Todd knew he had to say something reassuring.

"But you are in control of the situation Lianna," Todd responded. "*You* made the decision to go on leave. You also made the decision to contact Monique and pursue a counter attack on Noella. You have been the one to direct the conversations with Noella and she has always been the one to back down. You've got this! You really do Lianna," Todd said in a convincing tone of voice as they enjoyed their beer.

He smiled at her in a reassuring way and reached out and touched her cheek. She melted when his hand made contact, and Todd hoped he had convinced her of her strength.

She talked about her girls and how they were coping well with the current situation. She also shared about her ex-husband showing up on the same day of the break in and how he expressed concern for their safety. Todd suddenly became suspicious of Dave's motives and he also wondered just how Dave found out.

"I can't help but think that Dave knows more about the break in than he wants to admit," Todd said. "How do you think he found out?"

"Good question," said Lianna. "I wonder if Alfred thought I needed his support and maybe he called him?" Lianna thought carefully about it once again and decided she needed to ask Alfred.

She was now thinking about Noella and the proposed inspection at the school tomorrow. Was it just a threat or were they actually coming. She had to ask Todd what he thought.

"Noella said there's an inspection at Carlton tomorrow and asked if I had checked absolutely everything." Lianna then paused for a moment and thought. "Todd, do you think I need to be concerned? Should I do a walk through with my caretaker and/or facilities personnel?" She felt like she was being paranoid but she didn't want to underestimate Noella's deviousness.

"I think she's bluffing to be quite honest with you and this is just one more scare tactic she's using to intimidate you and waste your time. If she knew something, she'd probably be pretty blunt about telling you, especially at the eleventh hour like this." What Todd said made sense and it seemed to ease Lianna's concerns a bit.

"What you're saying makes sense, Todd. I am just full of doubt when it comes to her and her tactics," Lianna said with a frustrated tone of voice. "I don't want to waste precious time over something I couldn't control in the first place. Besides, Brad said that Facilities is on top of all this so I needn't worry right? They have my back …don't they?"

"Absolutely," Todd answered. "Now drink up. We should take a stroll along the river before it gets dark. They walked out of the bar and towards Lianna's car and as they came around the corner, they saw Todd's BMW … with two flat tires.

Lianna stared in horror at Todd's car then looked at him and said, "Todd! I am so sorry! I never thought they'd come after you too!" Lianna felt so badly and now their evening walk would be ruined.

Todd put his arms around her and pulled her close. "There's no way I'm going to let you take any blame for this Lianna. I'm starting to think that someone is watching us and I'm wondering if it's someone who doesn't want us to be together. For instance … a jealous ex-husband?"

Todd put the idea out there and wondered if Lianna might suspect Dave to be the one who did this.

"Not a chance," said Lianna. "Dave doesn't like me very much but he wouldn't do this to a complete stranger, especially you."

"You mean a complete stranger who is dating his ex-wife?" Todd asked, hoping to convince Lianna that it was a possibility. Lianna was silent for a bit, then Todd could see the wheels turning in her mind. *It couldn't be,* she thought.

"If Dave was still looking for revenge, he'd find another way to hurt me financially or something with the girls," Lianna said, trying to convince herself. "I just can't see him stooping to this level at all. He's got more class than that," she said, defending Dave's reputation.

"Ok…," said Todd. "I was just throwing it out there as a possible theory."

"Well, I appreciate your effort, Todd, but I don't think it's possible," she responded.

"Maybe you still have some feelings for him and your mind refuses to admit it," said Todd, suddenly realizing he'd crossed the line. He was frustrated about his car and now he was taking it out on Lianna.

"I think I better go Todd. The girls are going to be home and looking for supper." With that, Lianna turned without saying goodbye, got into her car and drove away, leaving Todd stranded with two flat tires.

****

The next morning, Lianna arrived at school early. She was there before everyone else and took some time to quietly reflect in her office. She looked at her 3 university degrees on the wall and many certificates from professional development courses and she felt proud of her accomplishments. She looked at the many books on her shelves that had given her practical knowledge as she learned to be a school leader and was thankful for every opportunity she had to be of service to children and their families.

She listened to her voicemail and one in particular caught her attention. It was someone named Brian from the Provincial Health Department announcing he would be at the school today. This caught Lianna off guard, but she said to herself at least it wasn't the asbestos inspectors.

She continued to work through some paperwork and finish some emails before staff began to arrive.

Teachers filed in one by one, some at least an hour before classes which was very common. At 7:45 AM, Patricia arrived and greeted her with a friendly hello.

"How are things, Ms. Lianna? Are you doing ok this morning?" she asked. Lianna knew Patricia had genuine concern for her and once again she proved to be the loyal and dedicated employee and friend Lianna knew she was.

"I'm fine," said Lianna, "but you know last night ... Todd's tires were slashed outside the lounge. I'm still upset about that, but I'm more upset that he and I aren't talking right now. I think I really need him."

"I understand," said Patricia reassuringly, as she hung up her coat and headed to her computer. "Mr. Todd is quite a catch!" and she smiled at Lianna knowingly.

"Thanks Patricia, I know you're absolutely right," Lianna replied. A moment later the security buzzer sounded and a voice came over the intercom.

"Hello, I'm Ziggy Donaldson from the health department. I'm here to do some testing."

"Ok, come on in," said Patricia and she let him in the front door. Lianna was concerned but was determined not to let this phase her or spoil her day.

"Good morning. I'm Lianna Monahan, Principal of the school. Are you here to check the lunch room facilities?" Lianna asked with a casual tone.

"No," Ziggy replied, "I'm here to test the water in the drinking fountains. There's been a complaint about impurities, and we had to respond quickly." He began to open his backpack and pulled out what appeared to be some kind of kit with test tubes. "I'll be conducting several tests throughout the school, but it shouldn't take too long."

"Complaint?" Lianna asked with a concerned facial expression.

"Apparently, someone has alerted us that the water supply pipes are over 50 years old and may be deteriorating. It's possible that some of the residue is being absorbed into the water and well … the rest is self-explanatory."

"Who lodged the complaint?" Lianna asked, irritated and upset.

"I'm sorry that's confidential information I can't share with you," said the inspector. "All I can tell you is that we are looking for possible lead contamination."

"Lead?" exclaimed Lianna, whose blood pressure had gone up substantially. "Why would you think you might find lead in the water?"

"Old pipes can start to break down chemically and some pipes years ago contained lead which can, with degradation, release lead into the water. Lianna looked at Patricia and then at the inspector in horror.

"I can't believe it," said Lianna. This is the inspection Noella warned her about yesterday. But it wasn't for asbestos containment. It was now about drinking water that children had daily.

"This has to be the work of Noella De Havilland," said Lianna to the inspector angrily. "And if you're not going to confirm that ... I'll find out for myself!

Chapter 23

The inspector was in the building for about half an hour, then signed out before he left. Lianna tried to talk with him but he refused to comment on his findings. She now had one more stressor to deal with and she was more worried than before.

The security buzzer sounded again and when Lianna looked at the video screen, a younger man stood outside the front door.

"Yes, can I help you?" Lianna asked.

"Yes, I'm Tony Barrenger and I'm here to meet with Lianna." His voice sounded friendly, and he moved toward the door.

"Come in Tony," Lianna said and she pushed the button to let him in. Tony entered the office with a big smile on his face. Lianna was ready to meet her replacement and put on a smile to make sure they started out on a positive note.

"Hi Tony," she began, "I'm Lianna. Nice to meet you." She reached out her hand for his.

"Likewise," Tony said, as he reached out to shake hers. "I wish it was under better circumstances. Brad has filled me in on the situation and I just want to say that I feel badly for you and what's going on. I really do.

It must be hard leaving the school with the lawsuits going on and I hope everything starts to get better. I hear this is a great school and largely due to your leadership."

"Thank you, Tony. I appreciate that," Lianna replied and she started to move slowly toward her office. "Please … let's start off in my office and I'll go through a few things you'll need to know."

Tony followed her into her domain, and sat down in a chair. "Nice office," he said. He looked at all her degrees and certificates on the walls and the many books on the shelves. He saw the picture of Dallas and Diane on her desk, and decided to ask about it.

"Your girls?" he queried.

"Yes," she quickly responded. "Dallas is 14 and Diane is 16 now. Time goes by so fast when you're a busy parent. Do you have kids?"

"Not yet," Tony replied. "Got married about a year ago. The two of us still having too much fun." He chuckled as he looked back at Lianna. "We want to travel a bit before we settle down and have a family."

"I hear you," said Lianna. "I wish I'd travelled a bit more before I had Diane. Once we started having kids it was so much harder. My parents weren't living here in town and most of our friends had their own kids. Not a lot of support available if we wanted to get away."

Tony sat silent for a moment as Lianna shuffled through a couple of files. "So, I guess I need to fill you in on the critical stuff, then we can talk more about the culture of the school etc. Is this your first time filling in as a principal?" Lianna asked him.

"I've done two or three assignments in the past couple years. They were short leaves. I barely had time to get to know the kids in each of those schools," Tony responded.

"Well … We have a very special school situated here in an affluent community," Lianna began. "The kids don't lack for much and they take some amazing vacations. It not uncommon for parents to pull them out for world travels and get them to do homework while they're gone."

"Sounds like the kids get everything they want maybe?" Tony asked, not fully knowing the context yet.

"I wouldn't say *anything*," Lianna replied. "Their parents work hard and they instill that work ethic in their kids. It'll become apparent to you as you get to know them better."

The conversation continued for a while, as Lianna showed Tony all her important files. They talked for some time, then toured the rest of the school as Lianna introduced Tony to the staff and students. He was impressed with what he saw, but it made Lianna sad as she thought about leaving everyone behind. She had to remember it was not forever, and that she'd be back again.

It was nearing the time for lunch and Lianna was trying to wrap a few things up. As the bell rang, Lianna saw Todd coming into the office and talking with Patricia. He had a bouquet of flowers in his hand and pointed toward Lianna's office. Patricia looked over her shoulder and nodded to Lianna, who nodded back with a smile. She motioned to Todd to come to her office, and they closed the door.

"I'm truly sorry, Lianna. I took my frustration out on you about my tires. I hope these will let you know how sorry I am." He handed her the flowers.

"It's a start," Lianna joked and smiled. "Have you had lunch, Todd?"

"Not yet," he replied. "It's in the car."

"Well why don't I grab my lunch from the fridge, and we can hop in your car and drive down to the river for a quick picnic," Lianna said with a smile. She reached for Todd's hand and then he kissed her before they left the office. "I'm so happy you're here, Todd," Lianna told him.

She grabbed her lunch, and the two of them left the school. They arrived at the river in minutes, and Todd reached into his trunk and grabbed a blanket for them to sit on.

They found a lovely spot in a shaded area and right in front of the beautiful river which flowed gently by. There were geese and ducks swimming in the water with their offspring, and the sound of crickets could be heard as they ate their lunch together. It was the perfect break from the worries of the day.

"Did you call AMA about your tires yesterday," Lianna asked him.

"Yes, and they towed my car to the BMW dealership where I paid an insane price for new tires," Todd replied, laughing as he spoke. He took a bite of his sandwich and watched Lianna as she ate the salad she'd prepared the night before.

"I don't know who is causing problems for us Lianna, but I sure hope it ends soon. I got a surveillance camera installed in my car ... which I should have done when I bought it," Todd said regretfully.

"Now I can see who approaches my car and they don't even know they're being watched. It's motion activated and I get an immediate notification if someone gets with 2 meters of my vehicle."

"That's great!" said Lianna. "If they try it again, I guess they'll be getting a visit from the police ... hopefully."

"And hopefully," Todd added, "there won't be another incident."

She knew he was still annoyed but not with her. He was determined to find out who was threatening them, however and as a man of action, doing his best to discover who it was.

The two of them finished eating then took a lovely walk on the path beside the river as they talked more about their relationship. Lianna still felt threatened by Noella and asked Todd to stay at her place for a few days.

"I talked to the boys and they said they'd be ok if I wasn't home for a few days. I'll check in on them, but they're pretty independent as well as responsible," Todd explained.

He was happy to help Lianna feel safe and would do anything for her now that they were in a committed relationship. "I'm so happy, Todd," she began, "I just feel bad that you have to go through all this with me."

"I know," Todd said. "But as I said before, I'm here for you, no matter what."

They paused their walk and looked out over the river from a high up vantage point. She turned to him and they kissed again, only this time for longer than in her office. Their bodies yearned for each other, and as they began to become more excited, Todd pulled away carefully and said, "I think we should get back, don't you?" He looked deeply into her eyes. She knew he was right but she longed to feel him all over her. She even looked into the treed area to see if there was a private spot, then shook her head asking herself what she was thinking?

"Yes. We should get back. But I want you so bad, Todd!" she seductively said to him as they began to slowly walk back to his car. They arrived to find the BMW intact, which was a relief for both of them. Obviously, whoever stalked them the day before was not following them again today.

They arrived in front of Carlton and Lianna kissed Todd before she got out and headed to the door. She swiped her fob and entered the building to see Brad and Chas standing near the office. They were talking to what appeared to be a facilities technician and Lianna's replacement Tony.

"Hello, Lianna," said Brad with a worried tone of voice. "How are you doing today?"

"Well, I had a lovely lunch by the river," she answered, "but somehow I'm thinking you have some bad news for me."

"I wish it was better news," said Brad. "Lianna, it appears that the health department has discovered some undesirable material in the water they tested."

"What!" said Lianna. "But Brad they were just here this morning," she said with disbelief.

"I know, but when a serious health risk is suspected," said Brad, "they act fast!" Brad took out a piece of paper which indicated numerous tests the inspector had done. "Look at line 24," Brad told her.

Lianna went down the page and the checklist of chemicals that allegedly could have been in the water. Beside the box on line 24 was the word *lead*, and a ppm amount which also was indicated as below safety standards. She couldn't believe what was transpiring.

"So, what do we do now?" asked Lianna, very concerned for her students. She looked at Todd who was equally shocked by the report. "Todd, what would you do in this situation?"

"Well for sure you need to block off access to the water fountains. I would announce to the school that they can't use them due to a plumbing problem." Todd thought carefully for a moment then said, "Maybe ask your staff to talk to the kids about bringing a full water bottle from home as well."

He was very practical about many things and Lianna admired this about him. "I'm sorry Lianna, I really need to go, but I'll call you when we're both done work today."

"I'll be right back," Lianna said to Brad as she walked Todd to the door. "This has to be Noella meddling again!" she said in a frustrated tone of voice.

"Remember," Todd reminded her, "This is beyond your control and not your fault."

Just then, they saw a TV media van pull up and a news crew was unloading equipment to go into the school. Lianna was determined to keep this out of the news. She promptly marched over to someone who looked like they were in charge.

"I'm the Principal," she said firmly to the crew who were now walking toward the front door. "How can I help you?"

"We're here to investigate a story about lead-poisoned water," said one female who looked official. "We need to ask you a few questions."

"No comment at this time," said Lianna abruptly, and she pointed to their van. "We're not inviting anyone in right now."

"This *is* a public building, is it not?" asked the reporter. "Are you refusing access to a public space?"

Then Lianna had to stop and think carefully about her response.

If she let them in the door, they might try to gather more information that may be damaging. They would see the fountains being covered and that would raise even more suspicion, and then of course the facilities person might be interviewed.

"The school act says I have a responsibility to protect the students in my building, and at this moment, you are a perceived threat to student safety. So bottom line …I'm doing my job under provincial law."

"How is it that a news crew is a threat to student safety Ms. Monahan? It *is* Ms. Monahan, isn't it?" the reporter smugly asked her.

"If you did your homework, you'd know the answer" said Lianna responding sarcastically. Suddenly, Noella came walking up the sidewalk of the school.

"These people are my guests," said Noella and I invited them to join me on an escorted tour of the school. I think it's within my right as a parent, don't you Ms. Monahan?"

"Just then, Brad looked out the front window and saw trouble brewing. He quickly rushed through the front door and said "I'm the chief superintendent of schools. Is there a problem Ms. De Havilland?"

"Hello Mr. Croskenheimer," Noella calmly said. "I was about to escort this lovely news crew - who are presenting no immediate threats or bad behaviour - into the school for a quick tour.

Brad knew what she was up to but was hesitant to refuse a parent access to her three children's school. He felt that his hands were tied.

"But they are a threat to student safety," explained Lianna. "Ms. De Havilland is seeking to find information that would not only hurt the students but also the reputation of the whole school as well as administration ... including you, Brad."

"What is the purpose of your tour, Ms. De Haviland," asked Brad.

"To show what an amazing school this is and what wonderful students and staff we have here." said Noella coyly. "And god forbid they should be subjected to any unhealthy conditions here," she added. Brad suddenly noticed that the crew was filming this exchange. "So, Mr. Croskenheimer ..." Noella began, "are you going to allow me access to my children's school, or do I need to go to the trustees, who I might add, are your bosses." Brad knew she had him over a barrel and reluctantly he turned to her.

"Ms. De Havilland ... you have 15 minutes, no interviews with staff or students, and you will stay in the hallways of this building." Brad was angry but felt he had no choice but to allow them access. "Any movement beyond that into classrooms or other spaces and I will call the police to escort you out. Am I clear?"

"Absolutely," said Noella in a sarcastic voice. "You see? Mr. Chief ... that wasn't so hard, was it?" She stared Brad in the eyes and then turned to the media crew.

"Follow me," she said confidently, and the news crew followed her into the building. "By the way, Ms. Monahan" she said to Lianna, "your services won't be required any more today!" And with that, Noella turned again and headed through the front door toward the main hallway.

Chapter 24

Lianna was fuming mad. Before she said anything she would regret, she stormed off to her office and shut the door. She noticed there was a voicemail on her office phone and wondered whether to listen to it. Hadn't she already had enough bad news today?

She decided she'd better see who left a message for her in case it was an urgent. She entered her pin and listened.

"Hello Lianna, this is Darren Matishyn. I'm afraid I have some difficult news. I wasn't able to get the trial date moved and so we will need to be in court next week… probably Tuesday. Can you please call me with a time we can get together to prepare for your statement and for some cross examination by the plaintiff." Lianna was very disappointed to hear this news and continued to listen.

"I'm so sorry…I tried to get it moved but the judge was unwilling to budge due to court schedules. Anyway, please call me at 403-627-7730. Thanks, Lianna" and the message ended.

Lianna wasn't sure how she was going to deal with all this but at least she was still going to see Todd on Friday night. She decided to call Todd and share the news.

"Hi Todd," Lianna began, "Thanks again for the lovely lunch by the river."

"It was amazing to be with you Lianna … in spite of everything else going on today."

Todd was sympathetic and decided to give her another listening ear.

"So, what's happened? Did the media get their way? Did Brad let them in?"

"I'm afraid so, Todd." she replied. "But he put some conditions on them. They're in the school but can't interview anyone and can't go in the classrooms. They're supposed to stay in the hallways, but I doubt they will. I'll check on them shortly." Lianna thought she better let Todd know about the court date before he came to stay with her Friday night.

"I have to go to court next week," Lianna said. "Darren couldn't change the date so I'm going full on in the civil trial on Tuesday. I think I'm going to have to put in some time this weekend which unfortunately might cut into some of our time together. I'm so sorry, but I can't change that." Todd was quiet for a moment and then spoke. "Then she owes us some of the time she's stealing from us this weekend." Todd chuckled in his familiar voice.

"I'd like her to pay that back in volunteer time in my school or better still … in Jail!" Lianna now laughed and Todd responded in kind. She talked further with Todd and they made arrangements to meet after work on Friday to acknowledge the beginning of her leave. They decided they'd go have a marvelous dinner at an expensive Italian restaurant, and she would pick up the tab this time.

Lianna decided to go check on her guests from the media and she wandered down the long hallway toward the library. She saw the group standing beside a huge fundraising display of cans and dry goods for the food bank and they were taking pictures.

It was good to see the focus of the media was a positive one. But suddenly her eye caught Noella standing around the corner talking to a student who wasn't her child.

They were beside the covered water fountain and she appeared to be asking him questions. As soon as Noella saw her, she hurried the student along toward the washroom but stayed behind to talk with Lianna.

"You know what the deal was!" said Lianna, glaring at Noella. "No interviews with students or staff." Lianna was ready to escort Noella out of the building.

"The child approached me with a question about the covered water fountains and so I talked to him. He seemed very afraid of something ... not sure what." Noella coyly explained. "I couldn't ignore the poor child. He seemed distraught so I offered my support."

"I think it's time for you and your crew to leave the building," Lianna told her. "Brad has given me full authority to remove you from the school if necessary and ... I'm not afraid to do it."

"What are you hiding Lianna?" asked Noella who was now being recorded by a reporter with a video camera. Lianna quickly turned to the reporter and was quite vocal. "SHUT! THAT! OFF!" She exclaimed as she took out her cell phone and began to call Brad on his private phone. Her voice could be heard down the hall by some students who looked at her from a distance.

"Look Lianna!" said Noella, "You're scaring the children! What kind of Principal does that? Especially one who claims to care so much about kids!" Lianna knew she needed to disengage as quickly as she could.

"You have 5 minutes to be out of my building Noella and that includes your sleazy entourage!" Lianna warned.

"Oh, it's *your* building now is it!" Noella stated, as she knew about the leave. "Last thing I heard was that you wouldn't be back after Friday."

"But I'm still here and I'm still in charge. Five minutes, Noella, or I'm calling the police to have you arrested for trespassing!" Lianna finished her sentence then turned and walked down the hall toward the office. She didn't look back to see what was happening but she heard movement from the video crew and assumed they were packing up. Lianna tried to regain her composure but it was so very hard. Her anger level had hit an all-time high and she was worried she wouldn't be able to calmly finish the day.

Noella and the group slowly followed down the hallway toward the front door and within 4 minutes or so, they were on their way out. Noella was the last one to leave and of course she had to make one more comment to Lianna.

"It looks like you've shown your true colours today Ms. Monahan." said Noella.

"I would hate to see some of today's media footage end up on the six o'clock news. It wouldn't be good for you, especially as you begin a very public trial next week. People don't like mean Principals ... and they certainly don't like ones who endanger kids' lives." Noella turned and walked away without waiting for a response from Lianna, which was probably a good thing.

Lianna turned and walked into the main office, frustrated once again as she picked up some mail from her mailbox.

She began filtering things out; the advertising vs those things that were really important. She thought about the events of the day again and she couldn't believe she hadn't totally lost her cool.

Just then, Tony came into the office after being in some classrooms to get to know the kids. "Hey Lianna, how's it going this afternoon?" Tony asked.

"Other than being ready to kill someone, not bad." Lianna responded. She then told Tony of the events following lunch and explained about the covered water fountains which was going to be a huge issue for him. At least Michael would be around to help with damage control and she was confident that things would work themselves out. As for her situation, she was very, very, worried!

****

Friday morning came sooner than Lianna wanted. Once again, she arrived very early to ensure that everything was in place and that Tony would have all necessary tools and documents to operate the school even in an emergency situation. She didn't like to think about the possibility of evacuation for an emergency however the staff was well prepared to handle events such as lockdowns and the like.

Lianna got caught up on her email and answered just about every necessary message before making her way out into the halls, which were still very quiet. It was 6:05 AM and no one had arrived in the building yet.

She walked past all the wonderful displays of student work, including what she felt were amazing works of art for elementary school age children. The staff took care to make sure all displays were well organized and that the quality of work on the walls was high.

As she walked the halls, she reflected on her early beginnings in teaching and her rise to leadership with encouragement from her mentors. It had been an amazing journey and she hoped it wasn't all coming to an end. Would she survive the civil trial and be exonerated from any wrong doing or would next week be the end of her career? She had to consider that it was a possibility she wouldn't return depending on the outcome of the trial. She decided to make this day one of the best she'd ever had in schools.

She continued to wander in the halls, then stepped into the library where she had so many amazing experiences with kids. She thought of all the times she read books to classes while their teachers went and prepared lessons.

She walked to the gym, where she spent hundreds of good times in assemblies and concerts as well as teaching children ball skills and how to do gymnastics.

This made everything worthwhile; to know that children learned amazing things from her and now that her leadership was making a difference in so many lives. In short, she was proud of herself and grateful for the opportunity to make the lives of others better. She decided at that moment, she would not allow Noella to take that away … no matter what the cost.

Chapter 25

It was an amazing day, just as she'd hoped. Lianna began with many reaffirming conversations with staff who stopped by her office to wish her well. The highlight of her morning was of course greeting students as they came through the doors, their smiling faces radiant and full of enthusiasm for the day ahead.

After the late bell, she went around and visited classrooms, talking with children and gathering energy from each and every one. At noon the staff surprised her with a special "going away lunch" which consisted of Mexican food and some delicious desserts. Michael gave a speech wishing her well in the upcoming challenges. The staff sang a song written in her honor by the music teacher, making her laugh as well as cry. Todd also dropped by and offered his best wishes, and as always, she was grateful to see him. He stayed for the noon celebration and then returned to his school.

The afternoon went well for Lianna, with nothing uneventful happening. She was however keeping her fingers crossed that nothing else would go wrong before she left.

She wrapped up the day saying goodbye to the kids, some of whom were crying as they hugged her and she always told them not to worry … she would be back.

Lianna went home early after work, after one last meeting with Michael and Tony. She wanted time to get ready for the wonderful night ahead with Todd, and she was determined not to let anything ruin it. She arrived home, greeted by Alfred in the lobby, then it was up the elevator to get ready for what she hoped would be a fabulous evening.

She entered the condo almost with a sigh of relief, setting her work bag down then going to her pillowy soft sofa to put her feet up. Dallas suddenly appeared around the corner, asking her mother how the day went. Lianna got up and hugged her for quite some time.

"Are you ok, Mom?" Dallas asked with concern. "Diane and I have been very worried about you."

"Yes, I am going to be ok, Dallas," Lianna said. "The trial is going to be on Tuesday next week, and I'm hoping it won't last too many days."

Dallas gave her mom another hug and then Diane came into the room. "You're home early," Diane said as she came to give her mother a hug. They held each other for a minute or two and Diane was reluctant to let go. "I've been so worried, Mom; I just can't explain how much." Diane added.

"Thank you, girls. This all means so much to me. Remember your mom is tough … I had to be in order to become a principal of a school!" Lianna chuckled and they all laughed together. "Tonight, I am celebrating myself and my success at the beginning of what I hope will be a short leave of absence. Yes, I have the trial go through next week, but for now, I'm celebrating the good things."

"That's great, Mom. And how are you doing that?" asked Dallas.

"Todd is taking me to La Bella Trattoria downtown," Lianna explained. "It's a fine Italian restaurant with many of my favorite dishes like Alfredo sauced chicken and Tortellini al Forno. I can't wait for dinner actually, but in the meantime, your mom has to shower and make herself beautiful."

"But you already are beautiful!" the girls both said almost in unison.

"Awwwwwe, thanks girls!" Lianna said, and she headed toward the hallway and her bedroom where she had a perfect ensuite shower and a huge sauna. There was also a soaker tub, but she didn't have time for that tonight. Tonight, the priorities were hair, make-up and finding a dress that would knock the pants off of Todd.

Lianna finished getting ready and the condo intercom buzzed. Todd was there to pick her up, and she felt like a teenager going on her first date. She almost ran to the intercom to talk to him then let him in the building.

"Hi Todd! Come on in!" she said enthusiastically. The buzzer sounded and Todd was on his way up.

Lianna stopped quickly in front of the full-length mirror by the door to check her dress and hair. She decided that she did the very best job she could of getting ready for what just may be the most important date of her current life. A moment later, there was a knock at the door and Lianna opened it with great anticipation.

"Hello," she said in a loving tone of voice. Before her stood a man who looked like he was dressed for his own wedding, with a sharp tuxedo which included a bow tie.

His hair was perfect and he had shaved his face to look smooth and inviting. Lianna took a long look at him before she said, "Come in, Todd. You look amazing! How are you tonight?"

"I couldn't be better!" he replied. "I've been looking forward to a night like this for so long."

"Me too," Lianna said as they walked in further. "Would you like a drink? I think we have time before the reservation."

"Sure," he replied and walked toward the balcony door. "Can we spend a little time with the amazing view while we indulge?"

"Absolutely! What would you like to drink? I have beer, whiskey, vodka, gin …"

"Maybe rye and coke," Todd responded as he opened the balcony door. He stepped outside to feel the crisp evening air, and took a deep breath. He admired the view, but the air was also fresh tonight.

Lianna made the drinks and brought them out to the balcony. She handed Todd his whiskey, raised her glass in the air and said, "Here's to us!"

Todd raised his glass to cheer and then added "and to justice!" He of course was referring to Lianna's situation and the court case ahead.

They stood talking for ten minutes or so and then realized they might need to leave to get to the restaurant due to traffic. Lianna grabbed her purse and moved toward the door.

"I'm leaving girls!" She called out as they opened the condo door. Both Dallas and Diane came running, and were a bit surprised to see Todd there, but they were happy to say hello. "Hi Todd," they said almost simultaneously.

"Hi girls," he responded. "What time should I have her home?" he questioned them facetiously.

"We were first thinking 9:00 P.M. but since you're dressed so nicely, you can have until 9:30 PM," said Diane jokingly.

"I thought her curfew was ten," Todd said, expanding the banter.

"I think we can let her off on good behaviour," said Dallas. "No later than midnight … what do you think Diane?" she asked her sister.

"Sounds good to me," said Diane. "Now run along kids! You don't want to be late!" Diane enjoyed joking with Todd and her mother, and particularly now that the relationship was more serious.

She "shooed" them out the door, and they headed to the restaurant for a much-anticipated delicious meal.

Todd opened the car door for Lianna, which is something Lianna had rarely experienced. All the men she had dated let her open her own door and it was a pleasure to be treated like a princess for once.

On the way, they spoke briefly about the following week then agreed not to talk about it for the rest of the night. Todd knew she'd have to prepare her testimony for the court on Tuesday, and that she'd need to meet with Darren sometime in the next couple of days.

They arrived at the restaurant on time, and were seated almost immediately in a quiet corner with no other table close by. The lights were dim and there were two candles on the table with a bottle of wine chilling in a bucket.

"I came here the other night and chose this table for us, Lianna," Todd told her. "I wanted a very intimate spot for the two of us to let go of the week and the worries, and just be together in a calm and relaxing environment. It had to be special for you."

"Oh, Todd, it's perfect!" Lianna responded, and she reached out for his hand. He gently held it and caressed it with his thumb as they gazed into each other's eyes. This was her first serious relationship since she parted company with her ex-husband and she was still a bit nervous, but now open to taking a risk for love once again.

"I'm so glad you like it, Lianna," said Todd lovingly, "and it couldn't be more perfect for me as well …especially with you!"

They sat quietly looking at each other for a moment, then the waiter came by and asked if he could pour the wine for them. He poured Lianna a little wine first, just for her to taste, and after she agreed to it with a nod, he poured some for both of them. Todd had ordered a sixty-dollar bottle of Chateau Le Freneure, which he also hand selected days before.

"You know, Todd," Lianna began, "we've been seeing each other for a few weeks, and it seems like we've known each other a long time. I guess we have, really, but it's now at a new level. I never thought I'd feel this way about a man again, but fortunately I was wrong."

"I know, Lianna, and I don't know how I lived without you before. To be honest, after Kate died, I swore I'd never love as anyone as much, and I didn't think it was possible. You've made me believe in love again; not that anyone could replace her, or your ex for that matter, but I see now that love is something worth taking risks for once again. I feel vulnerable, but at the same time, I'm so grateful to be with you. I really am." Todd looked like he almost had tears in his eyes, and looked away for a moment.

"This has all been worth it, Todd," Lianna replied. "I wouldn't want to be anywhere else or with anyone else in my life right now."

They each took another sip of their wine, and then looked at the menu which absolutely impressed them. After careful thought, they each selected an appetizer, a main course and a dessert.

The conversation continued during dinner and when all was said and done, they both reaffirmed they were meant to be together.

Following the meal, Todd made sure he paid the bill even though Lianna wanted to and she was so very grateful. She found a good man and she wasn't ever going to let him go.

After the bill was paid, Todd and Lianna headed to his car, again hoping the tires would all be intact. It appeared that all was as it should be, and Todd was relieved. Once again, he opened her door for her, and once again, she appreciated his gesture.

They headed toward her place and once on the freeway, Todd pushed the speed limit a bit. Lianna enjoyed a little rule breaking now and again, and she said nothing to him as he sped on the freeway. As they pulled up to Lianna's condo building, she thought she saw Dave's car parked down the block, but wasn't certain if this was actually his. Somewhere in her mind, she felt like she needed to know and decided to ask Todd to drive by.

"I know this is crazy, but do you remember when you asked if my ex, Dave, might have anything to do with our trouble?" Lianna carefully asked Todd.

"Yes I do, and I'm trying not to think about that right now, Lianna. Why do you ask?" said Todd.

"Well … don't be mad, but I think I saw his car parked down the street not far from here," she replied.

"And you want me to drive by to see if it really is?" asked Todd. He wasn't sure how he felt about this, but decided to do as she wished.

"Yes," she replied, "I know it's crazy but now I am thinking about what you said…you know…about Dave not liking us to be together."

"I understand what you're saying, Lianna." Todd responded. "I also want to know if it's his." Lianna was relieved that Todd agreed to check it out.

Before entering the parking garage, Todd turned the car around and headed in the direction Lianna showed him. As they got closer, Lianna was looking to see if there was a driver in the car. No one was in it. Todd slowed down and Lianna looked at the license plate. Sure enough ... it was indeed Dave's car!

Chapter 26

Lianna wondered where Dave might be. She didn't think he had any friends in the area, as he never lived in the condo, and she couldn't imagine a reason why he'd be around, other than to visit his girls.

"I'm going to text Diane," said Lianna, as she was now afraid Dave might actually be upstairs. "She'll tell me if Dave is there or if he's been by."

"Good idea," said Todd as he approached the underground garage entry. He borrowed Lianna's fob and they entered the garage and headed for Lianna's additional parking stall.

Lianna sent her text to Diane who was at home. Diane told her that Dave hadn't been by the condo and she and Dallas hadn't talked to him in days.

Lianna was now getting worried about why his car was parked down the street and her imagination was getting the best of her.

"Why do you think he'd be around, Todd," asked Lianna, who was very concerned and perhaps thinking she was a little paranoid.

"No idea, Lianna, but I'm sure there's some type of explanation for it. At least, I hope there is," said Todd hesitantly.

They parked the car and headed up to the condo where they found the girls sitting quietly watching a movie. Lianna had told them she had invited Todd to stay with them for some additional safety, and they both agreed it was a good idea.

"Hi girls! I'm home before my midnight curfew," joked Lianna. "And look at that! It's not even ten o'clock yet."

"What are you doing home so early?" Dallas asked. "Is something wrong?"

"Just the opposite," Lianna said, "We had a great dinner and now we just want to chill." Lianna moved over to where Todd had sat down, and she snuggled in beside him on the couch. "What are you watching?"

"It's a horror movie on Netflix," said Diane. "It's about a school principal who has people wanting to kill her because she's so smart and pretty!"

"Ha, ha!" said Lianna, as she looked at Diane. "So, it's a scary movie then?" she asked.

"Yah," said Dallas, "but it's a bit boring. Not enough blood!"

"I see," Lianna said. "And how much blood is enough?" Todd laughed along with them as they watched.

"I think I've had enough. I'm going to bed," said Diane and she looked at Dallas, hinting for the two of them to give their mom some privacy.

Dallas forced herself to yawn. "Ya … me too. It's been a long week." She looked at her mother knowingly and smiled. The two girls then got up and said goodnight to Todd and Lianna, then headed to their rooms.

"That was almost like they planned it," said Todd suspiciously. Lianna laughed, and looked at Todd who was also laughing. She loved his laugh and could listen to it all day. They continued to watch the movie for a few minutes and then Lianna had an idea.

"How about we take a drink out on the balcony and look at the city lights for a bit," Lianna suggested. Todd nodded and they got off the couch and moved outside. "Another whiskey, Todd?" Lianna asked. "Or would you like to switch it up?"

"Do you have a nice white wine?" he asked her.

"Absolutely!" Lianna replied. "I'll be back in two minutes." She went back inside the condo and poured two glasses of Lake Mahogany Chardonnay. She put some soft music on the bluetooth speaker and headed back outside. Todd was eagerly awaiting his glass of wine and looking up at the stars as well as the city lights which sparkled in the evening sky.

"Thank you, Lianna," Todd said as she handed him her glass of wine. He took a sip and said, "mmmm ... you have good taste in Chardonnays." He looked at her and smiled and she reached for him once again.

He responded by reaching for her hand and gently kissing it. Lianna was feeling very amorous, and Todd knew it. But the girls were in their rooms, and Lianna knew she and Todd would have to be discrete.

"What an amazing view," Todd said, continuing to hold her hand but also take sips from his wine. "You are lucky to have this place, Lianna." He looked out over the city lights which were amazing and the sky looked beautiful with stars everywhere.

"I agree, Todd," she said. "But you know what would make it even better?" She looked into Todd's eyes and he almost knew what she was going to say. "Having you here with me all the time," Lianna said and she moved in closer to kiss him.

They embraced each other, and soon their tongues began to explore each other's mouths, and with every motion, they wanted each other more than ever.

Todd caressed her bare shoulders and slid his hand under one strap, moving slowly downward and she began to kiss him even more passionately. They both knew they had to go to her room for more privacy and she took his hand and led him down the hall to her room.

They locked the door and quietly, they continued the kiss that started out one the balcony. She felt Todd's manhood becoming more expressive beneath his dress pants, but she wanted this to last longer.

She reached for the buttons on his shirt, and slowly opened each one, now kissing his neck as she unbuttoned them. He responded with low, guttural moans of delight, as she removed his shirt. She ran her hands all over his shaved chest and torso and with every caress he became more excited.

He turned her around and carefully reached for the zipper on the back of her dress, and ever so slowly, pulled it downward.

He lightly kissed her neck, now carefully moving the dress from her shoulders and she felt it fall to the floor. He continued to explore with his lips, and then made his way further down the middle of her back, nibbling gently to drive her crazy.

Ever so slowly, he opened the clasp on her lacy bra, then slid the straps off her shoulders, revealing her perfect breasts. He reached around with his hands, gently holding each one and running his index fingers over each nipple in a circular motion. She felt her womanly moisture increase and she turned her neck so Todd could kiss her mouth as he continued to caress her. Their tongues entwined, and Todd reached for her silk G-string, carefully tugging it toward her hips on each side.

"Wait," she said, as she turned and reached for his belt, opening it to reveal the top button of his pants. She undid the button and slowly pulled on his zipper, making eye contact with him all the time.

Soon his pants dropped to the floor and he stepped aside to free himself. His boxers showed Lianna his enthusiasm in the moment, growing with his passion as they continued to kiss.

They now stood facing each other, in only their underwear, and looking into each other's eyes, feeling irresistible desire. Todd picked up Lianna and carried her over to her bed, where he gently laid her down. He stood above her for a moment, as if waiting for her to invite his next move, and she suddenly said, "Yes, Todd."

He lowered his body, and kissed her torso, moving downward toward the top of her G-string. With his teeth, he tugged slowly … first the left side, then the right as she looked down and watched her panties moving toward her knees then her ankles, then finally gone from her body all together. Todd lowered himself to his knees beside the bed, grabbed her hips and pulled her closer to him.

He indulged in her forbidden fruit for several minutes, as she threw her head back in ecstasy. Suddenly, she said "Wait, Todd," and she sat up on the edge of the bed. She reached out for his boxers, and pulled them downward to reveal his perfect appendage. She felt compelled to bring him pleasure, and soon her mouth was fully engaged with his manhood. Todd threw his head back, feeling every second of pleasure, as Lianna showed him how much she wanted him.

He suddenly backed away, and taking her hands in his, he stood her up before him. "I want you, Lianna," he said as he kissed her passionately once again. "I had to slow down so we could experience the pleasure together."

"I know, Todd, and I want you so bad." Lianna moved herself into the middle of the bed and motioned for him to join. He moved over top of her and looking into her eyes, placed his engorged manhood close to her waiting cavern.

"Please, Todd," she said and she grabbed his buttocks, pulling him deeply inside. They were motionless for a moment, looking into each other's eyes and kissing with wild abandon. They began to thrust toward each other, moving their hips slowly in rhythm at first then with increasing fervor. Their breathing became heavier and soon Lianna let Todd know it was time. There was wild excitement as they reached their climax together, then collapsed in a passionate embrace that Lianna never wanted to end.

Soon, she was in his arms, laying on his chest, both completely satisfied and in love with each other. They were both exhausted, but in a euphoric state of mind. For a while, Lianna was able to forget all the stress of her situation and as the two of them fell asleep together, she imagined a life with Todd.

Chapter 27

Saturday morning came sooner than they thought, and Lianna woke up feeling safe and secure in Todd's arms. She looked at him, not wanting to disturb him, but somehow, he must have sensed she was watching him sleep. He opened his eyes and realized she was close to him, then he gazed into her eyes and smiled.

"Good morning sunshine," he said lovingly, and he gave her a kiss on the forehead. He continued to look into her eyes and was sure there was no other place he'd rather be than with her right now.

"Good morning, sweetheart," Lianna responded. "How'd you sleep?"

"Better than ever!" Todd replied as he gave her another kiss. "Your bed is amazing … but not as amazing as you."

"Awwwwwe Todd," Lianna began, "You know just what I need to hear don't you." Lianna couldn't be happier now that Todd was by her side and with everything going on, she was even more grateful.

"So, what do you say we get up and have some breakfast? I'm kind of hungry," she said with a caring tone of voice.

"Sounds good to me," Todd replied and he kissed and hugged her again. "Last night was amazing by the way," he added. Todd got up and Lianna once again saw his well-toned naked body. She was now rethinking the whole breakfast thing.

"Todd … I think the girls might both be gone to practice right now," she said suggestively. She looked at him and he knew what she was thinking. He stepped closer to the bed. "Do you think I might convince you to stay in here a little bit longer?" she asked with a sexy voice, hopeful he would oblige.

"You don't need to twist my arm, Lianna," Todd eagerly responded. Lianna reached out her hand and pulled him closer to the edge of the bed. She looked down and noticed that his enthusiasm was growing once again and she looked up at him with incredibly sexy eyes.

"You're so beautiful, Lianna," Todd said softly which drove her wild. "I just can't resist your charms."

With that, Lianna showed Todd once again how much he turned her on, and within moments, they were back in bed together. Because the girls were gone, they held nothing back and when they reached the peak of the moment, they simultaneously screamed in ecstasy, then collapsed together again.

They lay there for some time not saying a word but reveling in the amazing chemistry they found with each other. They knew they were meant to be together and nothing … not even Noella and the court case …could keep them apart.

****

Lianna and Todd spent the rest of the day enjoying each other's company. Lianna cooked an amazing dinner that night and the girls both loved it. They enjoyed having Todd around as he made them feel important. They had passed up the chance to go camping with their dad and were happy they did.

"Todd, are you sure you want to date our mother," Diane asked, playing devil's advocate a bit. "She can be very stubborn you know." She and Lianna both laughed and so did Todd. Dallas was quiet after this and Lianna was concerned.

"Are you serious Diane?" asked Dallas, who seemed to be worried that Todd would be offended. Todd knew he had to jump in.

"It's quite ok, Dallas," said Todd. "I'm not offended or anything. Diane is just checking on my commitment to your mom right now. It's normal for young people to do that with their single parents." Todd looked at Dallas and smiled and she smiled back.

"I guess I just don't want anything to screw this up for the two of you," Dallas said in a caring way. "We really like you, Todd."

"Why thank you, Dallas," Todd said to her. "I really like both of you as well." They continued to eat the delicious meal and had great conversation about many things the girls were interested in, especially sports.

"What made you become a Principal, Todd?" asked Diane. She was curious to see whether Todd and her mom had similar motivation that led them toward the job.

"I love kids and I want to make a difference in the world." Todd responded immediately. Diane was impressed, and surprised how quickly Todd replied.

"That's exactly what mom used to say," Diane responded. She looked at Lianna and said, "Isn't that right, Mom?"

Lianna smiled at Diane and nodded as she continued to eat. They finished the meal and then the girls went to their rooms to do homework and get ready for the week ahead. Todd and Lianna were cleaning up supper dishes and chatting in the kitchen.

"Your girls are amazing, Lianna," Todd said. "They must be so intelligent and I can tell they're your kids for sure!"

"Thank you, Todd. It hasn't been easy raising two daughters and especially while they're teenagers. Lots of hormones and drama to deal with but for the most part, they've been great. They work hard in school and with one or two exceptions, they've stayed out of trouble."

"You've done a good job, Lianna," said Todd. "I know some families who have it a whole lot worse and are fighting daily to keep their teens on the straight and narrow."

Todd came up behind Lianna and hugged her. He held on for a minute or so then he said, "Why don't you let me clean up the dishes and you pour yourself a drink and relax." He was so sincere and Lianna couldn't resist the offer. She knew how much he cared for her, even by this simple gesture. She knew he was a keeper.

"Are you sure Todd? There's a fair bit to clean up," she said to him.

Without hesitation, Todd grabbed her by the hand and led her to the sectional sofa that she liked so much and he sat her down. "You're not allowed to leave this spot for at least 30 minutes," he said. "Now what can I pour you to drink?"

"I have some of my red wine left over from dinner," she said, "it's on the end of the counter." Lianna lay back in her sofa and put her feet up. She was ready for a rest, but hoping she wouldn't fall asleep. Todd went to get her wine and brought it back immediately.

"I'm so lucky," she said as she reached out for his hand and kissed it gently before he returned to the kitchen.

Todd finished rinsing the dishes and loaded the dishwasher. He also washed a couple pots and pans by hand in the sink, which he was used to doing at his own place.

With two teen boys who always seemed to be running off to sporting events of their own, he was often left to tend to the dishes but didn't regret it. At least his boys were safe, busy, and out of trouble and that was worth it all.

He finally finished all the dishes and washed the counters and dining table. He even swept the floor which was something Lianna and her girls rarely did after dinner. Todd called out to Lianna, but there was no response.

He quietly crept into the living room where he found Lianna fast asleep on the sofa. She barely touched her wine. Todd decided to let her sleep for a while and quietly stepped out on the balcony to once again admire the city view.

He took a deep breath of night air and thought to himself how lucky he was to have a great career, a great family and now a wonderful woman in his life once again. He was a bit scared of the prospects, but he knew she was the right person to be his partner and that his boys would adore Lianna.

She slept for about an hour and was abruptly awakened by the ringing of her land line. She was startled at first then a bit disoriented, but moved quickly to go pick up the phone call.

"Hello?" Lianna said in a somewhat groggy voice.

"Hi Lianna, it's Darren." The board's lawyer was direct, passionate and a well-prepared individual and Lianna had great confidence in his ability.

"Hello Darren," she said quietly, not sure how she felt about what he was about to say. "Sorry, if I sound half asleep it's because I must have drifted off after dinner."

"So sorry to wake you, Lianna," said Darren, "but as you know, we have some prep to do before the trial Tuesday. Can you meet me at my office Monday morning? Shall we say 9:30 AM or so?" Lianna knew Darren had her best interests at heart and she immediately agreed.

"Yes, for sure Darren. I know how important this is and we need to position ourselves to beat Noella next week." Lianna was now speaking louder and with greater conviction as she thought about what lay ahead. Her dislike for Noella had increased ten-fold and she was now in warrior mode going into the trial which she now saw as a battle for her life and her career.

"Great!" said Darren. "I'll see you then. I might even buy you a coffee!" he added then said goodbye to her.

Todd had come in from the balcony, and had caught the last of her conversation with Darren. "So, when do you need to meet with him to prepare?"

"I'm meeting at his office at 9:30 Monday morning," Lianna explained. "He said he might even buy me a coffee." She smiled at Todd and he smiled back knowingly as they moved closer to each other. Todd hugged her once again and just held her for a moment without saying anything.

"You know I'm 100 percent behind you, Lianna," Todd said to her in a quiet and soothing voice.

"There's no doubt in my mind," she replied.

"Good!" Todd answered. "But for tonight, let's not think about anything or anyone else but us, ok?" he added.

"Sounds wonderful!" Lianna replied, and she snuggled closer to Todd on the sofa. They decided to turn on the gas fireplace, and together they sat, sipping fine wine and talking about their future. There was no room for negativity and certainly no room for …Noella!

Chapter 28

Sunday was uneventful, and after another passionate night together, Lianna made Todd an outstanding breakfast then they headed out for a bike ride by the river. It was a beautiful day with blue sky and sunshine, and they were both feeling that being together was the only thing they needed right now. They covered a long distance on their bikes, stopping once in a while to keep hydrated with water. They reached a cafe along the river and decided to go for coffee and a croissant, which they had heard were delicious.

"I think I'm going to have a chocolate croissant," said Lianna as she examined the entire menu. Chocolate was one of her vices. She didn't smoke and rarely ate things like potato chips, especially in the evening before bed. She was healthy and in good shape, but she couldn't resist the amazing chocolate croissants at the cafe.

"An excellent choice!" said Todd as he picked a blueberry one from the menu. "I love chocolate too, but these blueberry ones look amazing." They ordered and once they had their food, they headed out to sit by the river and talk.

They had much on their minds, but the focus today was the conversation about their families and a possible merge. They talked about their kids and their personalities and how they thought they would get along with each other.

"I know the kids are almost done high school, Todd, but I think I'd still like a house with a yard if we ever move in together," Lianna said.

"We've both lived in condos so long, maybe it's time to enjoy a yard with grass, with a deck and maybe some trees. Oh, and a hot tub too!" she added with a gentle question in her voice. Todd looked at her in an understanding way.

"I know what you're saying, Lianna, and even though the kids are almost done school, chances are they might even live at home if they go to university here. It's not such a bad idea," Todd responded. "I'd love to have a yard with flowers and maybe even a small garden to grow a few vegetables."

"Yes!" Lianna replied, feeling like they were on the same page about a house. "I'm so glad to hear you say that, Todd," Lianna said with relief in her voice. "My ex and I couldn't agree on how big the house should be though. It was always a bone of contention."

"How big a house do you want sweetie?" Todd asked. "We'd need room for 6 of us, right?"

"That's right, Todd," Lianna replied, "and maybe room for a little one too?" She smiled at Todd and he looked horrified. "Just kidding! I think we're both beyond that now ... but it's fun to think about," she added.

They talked for another hour or so and enjoyed the croissants immensely.

It was soon time for them to head back to the condo and for Todd to make his way home from there. Sunday night was always a busy time preparing for the week with some laundry and other miscellaneous chores to be done.

They reached the condo and locked up their bikes and headed upstairs. Todd had to collect a few things from Lianna's place, and then he would be on his way to see the boys. He gathered what he brought, but when Lianna used the washroom, she noticed there was one extra tooth brush. She wondered if it was just an oversight by Todd or whether he intended to leave one there.

"So ... Todd ..." she said smiling and holding up his brush, "is this staying here or going with you?" Lianna was hoping Todd would leave it behind.

"I don't know, Lianna. What would you like to see happen?" Todd asked, grinning and knowing full well what she would say. "If there's a problem I ..." Lianna immediately cut him off and responded.

"It stays!" she said emphatically. "And hopefully it will be used frequently for the next little while." Lianna looked into Todd's eyes and could tell he approved, and this made her very happy.

"Oh... and one more thing Todd ..." she went to the kitchen area and picked something up off the counter. "This is for you ... if you're ready for it." She handed him the key and the fob for her condo.

Todd was pleasantly surprised, but a little hesitant. "Are you sure, Lianna," he said, looking deep into her eyes to see the truth. "I am ready, but are you?" he asked, not trying to cast doubt but just to confirm her decision.

"One hundred and ten percent!" Lianna replied and she came over to hug him. They embraced for a moment, then began to kiss, which lead to more. "The girls won't be home for a couple hours," she said, half kissing and talking at the same time. She looked into his eyes and he knew what she wanted next. He followed her lead and soon they were behind closed doors and, on their way, to more passionate moments together.

****

Todd went home and the girls arrived about an hour later. It gave Lianna time to reflect on the upcoming week and her meeting with Darren the next day. She thought about many scenarios and possible responses, and she decided that the bottom line was to be truthful and only reveal what was absolutely necessary. The girls came home and they all ate supper together. They were understanding and considerate of their mother's situation and tried to keep things light at dinner.

"You know, Mom," Diane said, "This could all be over by Wednesday."

She gave her mother a hopeful look and Lianna reached out to touch her daughter's hand. She wanted it to be over by Wednesday, but somehow Lianna doubted that it would. "Does Noella still have 2 lawsuits against you," asked Diane.

"Just one against me personally and one that involves me and the school board," Lianna answered. "It's pretty complicated but I'm sure things will become clearer as the trial progresses." Lianna tried to stay calm while she spoke so the girls wouldn't get upset. She knew they hated Noella and that wouldn't change. She just hoped they wouldn't do anything to jeopardize her situation at the trial.

They talked for a while, and the girls went off to bed. Lianna looked down over her balcony and was sure she saw the car that followed her a few days earlier. It was parked in front and across the street from her building. This brought her blood pressure up as well as her stress level which she didn't need right now. She decided to go down the elevator and out the front door, her heart racing all the while.

She looked across the street to see if the car was still there but it had taken off. Suddenly from out of nowhere her ex-husband Dave pulled up in front. He lowered his window on the passenger side and said "Hi beautiful. What brings you out here on such a fine evening?" He looked at her and smiled but she didn't smile back. She didn't trust him, and she made that clear, but he tried to assure her that his intentions were still good. After all, he was the father of her children.

"What are you doing here Dave?" Lianna asked, now very suspicious of his presence. She stared at him to almost make him feel uncomfortable and he was silent for a moment, as if trying to think of an excuse.

"I was just over visiting a friend up the street," he said. "He was someone I went to high school with years ago. His name is Boyd."

"I see," replied Lianna, "and what kind of a car does Boyd drive?" asked Lianna. Suddenly, Dave looked very nervous, and he looked away for a second. He then got out of the car and came around to the sidewalk.

"I think it's a blue BMW or something like that. I've only seen him drive it once," Dave responded. Lianna thought he still looked nervous and he wondered if there might be a connection between the car she had seen and Boyd … if in fact Boyd did exist. If he was someone Dave made up, then could it have been Dave driving the car from across the street? She continued to imagine and try to put things together. She asked herself if Dave was angry enough to cause problems for her. Lianna also wondered if Dave had talked to Noella at all and she decided to confront him.

"Ok, Dave …" Lianna began, "let's play a truth or dare, shall we?" She looked him straight in the eye. "Do you know someone named Noella?" she asked directly.

"Yes, I think so. She's the woman from your school, right? Didn't she raise a whole ton of money a few years ago when you first got to the school?"

"Yes, she's the one." Lianna replied. "Do you remember her?"

"I think so," Dave replied sounding a bit nervous.

"When was the last time you saw her Dave?" Lianna asked him pointedly, and hoped for an honest response.

"Quite a while ago," Dave said. "Oh, actually ... I did run into her at the grocery store a few weeks ago. She asked me how you were doing."

Lianna lived with Dave for years and could now tell that he was trying to hide something. She had to decide whether to push the issue or leave it.

"Oh really," said Lianna, "and did she sound genuinely concerned about me?" Lianna was starting to get stressed and she wasn't sure if she really wanted to know the truth from Dave. He looked away before answering and she knew she wouldn't want to hear any more about their conversation.

"It was small chit chat you know Lianna ... just casual." Dave seemed like he was trying to minimize his involvement with Noella.

"And have you talked to her since?" Lianna asked him. She was now digging deeper for possible connection between Dave and Noella and honestly hoped there wouldn't be any.

"No," Dave replied quickly. Again, he looked way and Lianna felt like he was lying.

"You know, Dave, if I find out you had anything to do with my lawsuit,

I will see to it that you can't have access to the girls. Actually, if they find out you were involved, I won't even have to go to court ... the girls will just refuse to see you ... period!" Lianna was now very angry and Dave could easily tell.

"I assure you, Lianna, I am not involved in any way. Don't you know me better than that?" Dave was now trying to deflect some guilt Lianna's way and she didn't appreciate it.

"Whatever Dave! You haven't changed much and why would I think you could." Dave turned and walked away at this point and Lianna didn't really want to talk to him anymore. He got into his car and drove away in the direction he came from.

Lianna quickly ran down to the underground parkade and got into her car. She raced out of the garage and turned to follow Dave's path. She drove a couple blocks, and soon saw his car again. It was parked right behind the car from across the street - the same car that had followed her a few days earlier.

Chapter 29

Monday morning came quickly and Lianna prepared herself to go to Darren's office. She decided to dress up as she always felt better when she did. Lianna was a proud woman who always wanted to present her very best self and being her best with Darren was no different. This time however, her career could be on the line. She told herself that she would be true to herself and her agenda, but would be flexible if it came to saving her job. She had the girls to think about, so she needed to come out with a win on this one.

She had a good breakfast and said goodbye to her daughters before exiting the condo. She greeted Alfred as she usually did, then made her way to the parking garage.

Now she always had an eerie feeling before getting to her car that something might be wrong. Today everything was fine, and she got in and left the parking garage.

As she turned onto the street, she looked into her rearview mirror and saw the blue car again. It was hard to tell who was driving as even the front window was tinted.

Lianna decided she'd had enough and she stopped dead in the middle of the street, got out of her car and started walking toward the vehicle which could not back up as someone was behind them. She knew it was crazy, but walked up to the side window of the car and tried to look in.

She knocked several times on the side window but the driver wouldn't open it. The car behind it was honking their horn now and getting impatient so it finally backed up and sped past Lianna, and as it did, the blue car quickly backed up and did the same. Lianna yelled "COWARD!" As it drove past, and she quickly got back into her own vehicle.

She sat for a moment after pulling over to regain her composure and said to herself that what she did was a dangerous and crazy thing to do. She decided to call Todd using her bluetooth and started driving toward Darren's office.

"Hi Todd, it's me," Lianna said as Todd picked up his cell. "I think I just did a crazy thing. Do you have a minute?"

"For you, always." Todd replied. "And if I didn't, I'd make one for you. What's up?" he asked.

"You won't believe what I just did." Lianna told him. She explained what happened and he was surprised.

"Ya, Lianna, that could have gone south quite quickly. Are you ok?" Todd was very concerned about her and needed her to know that.

"I'm fine now, Todd. I was just so angry that this car was following me again and I had to push back," Lianna explained. "They needed to know that I'm clearly aware of what they're doing. I just couldn't get an ID on the driver though. They got away just in time. Crazy thing is that their windshield was also tinted and I couldn't even see in the front."

"I hate to say this, but you could have been shot, Lianna," said Todd with concern. "We don't know exactly what kind of people we're dealing with here but they're not very nice. It was risky but I understand why you did it. I don't know what I'd do if I lost you sweetheart!" Todd was genuine and not angry with Lianna, but he didn't feel she realized the huge risk she took.

"I know, Todd. As a mother of two I should have never put myself at risk like that. It was crazy and not very smart!" Lianna was regretful as she realized how much Todd cared for her.

"I hope you won't do anything like that again, honey," Todd implored, and said it with love and sincerity. "Maybe you could call the police if they follow you again, but don't stop on the road."

"You have my word," said Lianna. "Never again!" she reassured him. Todd was relieved she was ok, but he had to deal with an urgent matter at his school.

"I'll call you in a while to find out how your meeting with Darren went," he said to reassure her. He was right - she should never have done what she did and she was grateful that no harm came to her. She had to focus on her strategy with Darren now and didn't have time to rehash her decision any further.

She arrived at Darren's office moments later and sat in the waiting area. While she did, she checked her work email (even though she was on leave) and her mind drifted back to the school she left behind. She hoped that things were running smoothly, but she also had a sense of relief that she didn't have to deal with work at least until the trial was over.

"Hi Lianna," said Darren as he met her in the waiting room. "Welcome to my office!" He was cheerful and smiling at her, which made her feel more comfortable. "Are you ready for this?" he asked.

"As ready as I can be," Lianna replied, as she walked down the hallway with him. "I can't wait to get this trial over with so I can get back to work again," she said, somewhat frustrated that she even had to go through this.

"I understand," said Darren as they entered his office. "Please … have a seat," he said as he pointed to a leather chair across from his desk.

"Nice office," said Lianna she looked at the art work on the walls and several of Darren's degrees and credentials.

She was especially impressed with his degree from Harvard Law as well as his Juris Doctorate degree, which he got from Stanford. "I didn't know you went to Harvard," she said, impressed with Darren's past.

"Well, I'm glad you know now," said Darren, "But truth be told, I could have gone anywhere, and still been a great lawyer. Harvard just made it easier to get a job. I bet you're wondering why I am working for a school board given that I went to Harvard and could probably have made more money with a private firm," he added.

"I try not to worry about things like that, but I am curious," Lianna told him.

"Well, it's a long story but I'll give you the main reason … I wanted to make a difference in public education," Darren began. "My siblings were privileged to go to any University in the world after going to private schools. I was adopted and went to public school all my life, and I saw how much the system needed more resources. I didn't think so much of it when I was in high school, but I realized it much more when I went to public university in Canada."

"Luckily, my parents decided to fund my education when I got into Harvard and for that I'm grateful, but I feel I owe my success in Harvard to my roots in public education and want to give back to the system that raised me. Does that sound like a lot of BS?" He smiled and looked at Lianna for an answer.

"As a matter of fact," Lianna began, "I really admire you for that, Darren. There are not many lawyers around that would think like you, as they'd probably be after the glamour of law practice after a Harvard degree. You're different, and that's what makes me even more thankful that you're representing my interests. I know you'll do your very best … for humanitarian reasons," Lianna added, somewhat facetiously, but with good intention.

"Thank you, Lianna," Darren said. "It's good to know I have your confidence behind me as we go to trial." He opened a file that was sitting on his desk and reviewed all the information with her.

"So, you believe she harassed you outside of the workplace as well, do you?" Darren asked her.

"Yes, I don't have proof that she was behind the break in at my condo or the car stalking, but I have strong suspicion." Lianna was honest about her situation and Darren appreciated her candor.

"Is there anyone else who might want to hurt you or your reputation," Darren asked pointedly.

"Well …" Lianna hesitated, "there is my ex-husband - the father of my girls - but I don't think he wants to hurt me because it would mean hurting our children as well. Besides, if I lost my job, he'd have to step up and support them more."

"Or go for custody …" Darren thought carefully before he said that. "I'm sorry to say it, but he does have something to gain personally from your demise," he added. Lianna hadn't thought about it in those terms yet, but now it was starting to make sense why Dave seemed to be hanging around coincidentally on several incidents. She shared this with Darren and he agreed that Dave may have a connection.

"I think I may need to subpoena him and ask him a few questions, Lianna. There may be more to his alleged concern than you think." Darren was now very suspicious of Dave's motives and it was plausible that the guy was seeking personal gain if Noella was successful.

"Ok. Let's get back to Noella for a minute," Darren began. "She's accusing you of negligence in disregarding asbestos reports done by facilities. Did you see those reports?"

"I asked to see them, and we did a walk through the building soon after I arrived a couple years ago," Lianna said. "I believe the person's name was Darmeet Singh, the area supervisor at the time. We walked through the entire building and examined each area where asbestos was a possibility in the walls, ceilings and tile. He assured me that all of it was covered and no exposure remained."

"Did he sign another document to confirm that?" Darren asked.

"I believe he said he'd email a confirmation to that effect. I'd have to go back in my emails quite a way to find it, but I think I saved it," she said.

"Hopefully you did, because that, together with Darmeet's report should be enough to exonerate you from any wrong doing," stated Darren confidently. He was happy to hear Lianna give him that information.

"I hope so," said Lianna. "I remember Darmeet … what a nice man. Hopefully he still works for facilities," she said calmly.

"Speaking of facilities Lianna, how well do you know Mitch Mason" Darren asked.

"Why do you ask?"

"His name has come up several times and Noella seems to know him quite well for some reason. Not sure how." Darren responded. "I believe he is on the list of Noella's witnesses."

"Not sure why," Lianna replied, and she was more worried about the trial knowing this.

"I don't think we really have to worry about him," Darren told her. "You are in compliance with all the facility department's policies. I've looked through all their documents."

"Now let's talk about your ex again," said Darren. Did I hear you say he just showed up soon after you discovered the break in at the condo? To see if you were alright?"

"Yes. That's what he said. He was vague about how he found out and didn't want to tell me exactly. I was a bit suspicious at that time, but I kind of brushed it off."

"I see. And you say you were followed a couple times when you were in your car correct? But not by your ex-husband's car am I right?" Darren was starting to put a theory together but Lianna still wasn't sure where he was going with it.

"Correct," Lianna said. "And one time, my ex showed up just shortly after I observed the car parked close by."

"That was the blue car …" Darren confirmed.

"Yes," said Lianna again.

"So … your ex seemed to know your comings and goings mysteriously or coincidentally."

"What are you saying, Darren?" she asked a little worried.

"I think Dave has rigged up some surveillance mechanism that you don't know about," Darren said reluctantly "… either cameras or an audio device … and probably in or around your condo."

This thought worried Lianna, and as she thought about it, Dave had the capacity as a person who was very good with technology, to set up some things like that without her knowing.

"Oh … my…God!" Lianna said with a horrified look on her face. "He might have been watching us or listening for some time now!"

"That's entirely possible, but very creepy if you ask me," said Darren. "Listen, I know someone who can 'sweep' your condo for devices. If there's something there …he'll find it. I'll call him right now if you'd like."

"Please do," said Lianna. "Are we ready for tomorrow, Darren?"

"All you need to remember is to be honest." Darren said. "If you haven't done anything outside regular protocol, and I don't think you have, everything will be fine. Let's wrap up here and I'll call my techie friend.

"Thanks so much Darren," said Lianna. "You're amazing!" And with that Darren called his friend in the surveillance equipment business who agreed to meet them at her condo.

Chapter 30

Lianna was nervous but also felt secure in knowing that if some spying devices were there, they would be found. They met Darren's friend Steve at the main doors and together they went up the elevator.

"Thanks for coming on such short notice," said Lianna. "My trial is tomorrow and we may need the evidence to counter the argument of the plaintiff."

"My pleasure," said Steve as they reached her floor. "I just hate when people become victims of privacy violations and so on. It makes me sick!"

"Well, I hope you find nothing but, in some ways, I would like to show culpability, especially for the woman who has made my life hell for the past couple of weeks." Lianna was drawing sympathy from Steve as she explained.

"I understand," Steve said. "I've personally been through some issues myself and it's terrible. Let's hope all is well up there." They continued to Lianna's floor then down the hall to her door on the right. Darren followed Steve into her place and Lianna put her things away. "I think I'll start in here," said Steve, as he looked around the living room. "Nice place, Lianna!" Steve said as he unpacked some equipment to check the condo out. "This should only take about 15 minutes."

Steve had an electronic scope and a wireless device that he waved it around in the air. He looked under the sofa and inside cabinets as well as checked out nick knacks on the mantle. He seemed very thorough and Lianna was impressed. After finding nothing in the living area, he decided to go to Lianna's bedroom. "I hope you don't mind Lianna. I know it's hard when a stranger goes through your bedroom and I …"

"Say no more, Steve," she interrupted him and smiled. He began the scan of the room and soon his machine was beeping, slowly at first, then increasing in speed as he moved toward the dresser. "I think we have something here," he said. He brought the scope close to a photo of Lianna and the girls, and then he shut off the scope. "How long have you had this?" he asked and began to immediately disable and disassemble the camera.

"I've had it since my ex moved out. He wanted me to have it and insisted that I keep up in my room." Lianna spoke and immediately she remembered the day he left and his insistence that she have the photo and frame displayed. "That's why he wanted me to have it. What is it? What's the device?" Lianna asked.

"There's audio …" said Steve, "and …." he hesitated, "unfortunately, there's video as well."

"THAT CREEP!" Lianna immediately yelled and then apologized for her outburst. "I feel so violated! I can't believe he'd do that!" She was beyond angry, and Darren tried to calm her down.

"Maybe we can turn this into an advantage, Lianna," Darren said. If we can establish a connection between Dave and Noella, then we can not only win this case, we can press charges against both of them. Noella won't have a leg to stand on."

Lianna was enthused by this although very much felt her privacy was invaded beyond repair. She sat down to contemplate the possibilities of Dave having footage of her in her room and also … her and Todd, which horrified her even more! "I can't believe it! I'm dumbfounded and speechless. I need to call the police!" she said.

"Wait!" said Darren. He probably knows by now that we've found his camera and mic. I can have Steve testify to what we've found." He thought for a moment. "Steve, can you trace the address of the camera back to a computer by chance."

"Yes, maybe if I do it right away," Steve replied, and he took the frame and accessed the camera with his computer. With sophisticated software, Steve was able to identify the IP address of the source and further GPS information. "Got it!" said Steve as he continued to look at the camera.

"Any chance of telling what may have been recorded, Steve?" said Darren.

"Not really possible, Darren," said Steve. "But if we can find the computer, which is a long shot, then we will be able to tell. But there is one other thing and I'm not sure you're going to like it.""

"What is it?" Lianna asked, fearing that things would get worse.

"Video footage was going to a second IP address somewhere else. Let me see if I can pinpoint a geographic location or owner. It's going to take a few minutes, but I think I can do it.

Lianna now feared for her privacy and safety even more. Who else could be involved in this breach and what were they after? After about 7 minutes, Steve said, "Bingo! I've got it! Wow! Did you say you work for the Board of Education?"

"Yes, I do. I'm a school principal."

"Well, I'm afraid that someone in your organization is also involved.

The IP address, while initially hidden, is now showing it's a school board owned computer," said Steve hesitantly. Lianna looked at him in disbelief,

"Are you sure, Steve?" she asked?

"99 percent sure, Lianna. And …" Steve checked his equipment again. "Now it's 100 percent," he said as he hit more keys on his keyboard.

 "You can call the police right now, or you can keep this under wraps and confront your ex and insist on seeing his computer.

Then if he refuses, tell him you are going to the police at that point. Either way, I think you've got him."

"Can we go find him now?" asked Lianna, eager to get the ball rolling.

"It's up to you, Lianna. Are you ready?" asked Darren.

"Absolutely," Lianna began, "but if I go crazy, I need you guys to hold me back. I'm going to try to regulate my emotions, but if I have trouble, I need you to have my back. Ok?"

"For sure you can count on us, Lianna," said Darren.

"Let's head on out then," said Steve as he walked toward the door. They left the condo and Darren offered to drive the 3 of them. Within a couple minutes, they were on their way to Dave's place.

****

They arrived at Dave's place about 10 minutes later. "I have some experience confronting people in situations like this," said Steve. "Do you want me to start the conversation?"

"Maybe if we make this seem more official, he'll be less likely to cause trouble. If he asks if I'm a cop I'll just say that I'm with the authorities, and he's under investigation for breach of privacy," said Steve.

Lianna thought this was a good idea and agreed to let Steve do the talking at first. She would follow his lead when it was her turn to confront Dave and she felt comfortable with this. Lianna decided to go up the front steps first, then stepped to the side and let Steve center himself on the landing. They rang the doorbell and waited for a moment before the door slowly opened.

"Well, well, look who we have here!" Dave said. "To what do we owe this pleasure?"

"Are you Dave Monahan?" Steve asked abruptly.

"Who wants to know?" Dave replied, in an irritated way. He suddenly put on an angry face but Steve didn't flinch or appear afraid.

"My name is Steve and this is Darren, Lianna's lawyer. May we come in?" Steve didn't expect Dave to be cooperative but he did agree and invited the 3 of them inside. "Thank you," said Steve as they entered.

The place seemed dark and a bit dingy with 70's decor and it didn't smell very pleasant.

"Excuse the mess," said Dave as he moved further into the living room. "So, what is this all about? Has Lianna finally come to her senses and wants to get back together?" Lianna was incensed with this question and it was everything she could do not to comment.

Web of Lies

"We found a camera at Lianna's that records video and audio, and it was in the frame of a photo that you gave her. What do you have to say about that Dave?" Steve asked, looking him straight in the eye.

"That's ludicrous!" said Dave. "Do you have this frame?"

"Of course we do" began Steve, "and I have the technology to trace it's transmission to the source computer which is here at your address according to GPS coordinates." He kept looking at Dave who seemed to look away every few seconds. Lianna was also staring at Dave and wanted to know why he would do such a thing.

"You're lucky we haven't called the police!" said Lianna as she was now ready to engage in confronting Dave directly. "Why would you do such a thing Dave?"

"I'm sorry, Lianna," said Dave apologetically. "I truly am. You've caught me, and I can't deny it."

"So now you have a choice to make," said Lianna. "You can bring us your computer and show us any footage you have or I can call the police right now and you can show it to them!"

She spoke angrily and very pointedly to Dave and he knew she was serious. "What is it going to be?" she said. Dave thought for a moment then responded.

"So, if I turn over any video I have, you won't press charges? Are you willing to sign an agreement ensuring that?" Dave asked. He looked at Lianna and then at Darren.

Lianna looked at Darren and he nodded his approval for the agreement, and then Lianna said, "Yes, but I need to take your laptop too. The girls could use another one in the house." Dave wasn't sure he wanted to just give it up but he reluctantly agreed.

"I'll write up the agreement right now. Go get the laptop, Dave." Darren spoke firmly and directly. By the way, she'll need your password immediately to open the computer and get access."

Dave went and got the laptop from his home office and brought it to Lianna. "Start it up," she told him, and he complied. In a moment they were at the login screen. "What is your password? I'll enter it," she demanded. Dave told her the password and she now had access.

She browsed around for a while, then she asked Steve, "How do I find all video files at the same time?" Steve showed her a quick way to search all video formats and also how to get into the camera software that Dave had used.

She found video footage of numerous times she'd been with Todd, and various conversations she'd had with others on the phone.

"You're a sick man, Dave!" she said as she deleted numerous intimate moments that were recorded. "Were you watching these on a regular basis?" she asked.

Dave nodded and was very embarrassed. "I'm so sorry, Lianna. I just couldn't bear to live without you … or at least being able to see you in some way. I really was in love with you … maybe still am," Dave said as some tears came to his eyes.

"Well, any feelings I ever had left for you are completely gone now!"

she told him. Lianna kept deleting video after video and finally came to what she felt was the last of the files. "Are there any more on this computer? Or any copies anywhere else?" she asked him.

"That's everything," Dave responded.

"What about cloud back-ups?" Steve asked. "Take us to those, right now." Dave logged into his one drive and found the back-ups which Lianna went to delete. "Now tell us who else is involved and receiving video and audio feeds? We know there's another computer, and that it belongs to the school system."

"That's insane!" exclaimed Dave who seemed genuine in his response. Steve stared at Dave for about ten seconds.

"He's telling the truth Lianna. He doesn't know who it is." Steve replied.

"How do you know that, Steve?" she asked urgently.

"The feeds are independent, and each one is encrypted so can't be seen directly by shared computers. He's telling the truth unless he's talked with the other owner somehow."

"Alright Dave, if you know something, now is the time to fess up!" Lianna said with an angry tone.

"I swear on the lives of my children, Lianna, I don't know who it is." Lianna looked into his eyes and because she knew when he was lying, she was convinced he was being truthful.

Steve said, "Wait, Lianna. We need at least one or two for evidence in case he goes against his agreement down the road." Steve pulled out a flash drive he carried with him and copied 3 files for Lianna, which she thanked him for doing.

"Here's the agreement for you both to sign," Darren began. "It states that Lianna agrees not to press charges for any recorded audio or video from Dave's camera illegally installed in her condo, and that in turn, Dave agrees to ensure that no further copies exist on any device he owns.

He also agrees to turn over ownership of this laptop immediately, and to refrain from any further surveillance involving Lianna or her daughters. Is that everything you wanted to see Lianna? Dave?"

"It's not what I wanted, but I guess I have no choice," said Dave.

"It's perfect, Darren," said Lianna. "Where do we sign?"

Darren showed each of them where to put their signatures and Steve witnessed the document for them. Steve was still visibly upset, but Lianna appeared to be satisfied with the outcome of their efforts.

"Anything else we need here, Lianna," Darren asked. He looked at her as if to say that maybe they should go.

"I think we're done here, Darren, but I just need a moment alone with Dave," She replied.

"Are you sure," Darren asked and Lianna nodded. "We'll be just on the other side of this door if you need us," he added.

"Thank you!" Lianna said as Darren and Steve exited through the front door. Lianna wasn't sure exactly what more to say, but she knew she had to keep her cool.

"Just one question Dave…" Lianna paused. "If a man did this to either of your girls, what would you want to see happen to him?"

She stared at Dave who looked away and couldn't make eye contact. "What would you want to do to him, Dave?" she added. He was silent and couldn't offer a response.

"Again, I'm so sorry Lianna. Please forgive me," Dave said remorsefully.

"You'll be lucky if your girls want to see you ever again," Lianna warned him and she turned and walked out the door.

Chapter 31

There was media outside the court house as Lianna and Darren pulled up. Darren's driver opened the door for them and they were immediately surrounded by reporters. "NO COMMENT!" He calmly said to them as he tried to protect Lianna and Darren from having cameras in their faces. They made their way to the steps of the court house and entered the building. They needed to go through security which involved scanners and metal detectors much like in an airport. Lianna put her bag into a plastic tray which passed through an x-ray type scanner to ensure she had no weapons or dangerous electronic devices.

They took the elevator to the second floor where there were several court rooms as well as passages to the judges' chambers. Darren was greeted by several colleagues as they walked toward the end court room, and he seemed to know many people who worked in the facility.

They entered the court room, which had a gallery at the back and desks near the front where the lawyers and clients sat during the trials. Darren led Lianna to the front and they sat down on the defendant's side of the room. The trial would begin in ten minutes and Darren and Lianna talked quietly to review some of the questions she might be asked. She was confident that telling the truth would bring her success in the trial, but she had some mild reservations.

Lianna heard a commotion and turned to look back at Noella entering the court with 3 lawyers. She was dressed to the nines with perfect hair and her make-up was flawless. She wore high stiletto heels that matched her dress which looked like it was recently purchased on Rodeo Drive in Beverley Hills. In short, she looked powerful and extremely well put together. She and the lawyers sat down after Noella scowled at Lianna and Darren.

Darren had his files and notes in front of him and she was convinced he was ready for anything. Suddenly the door at the front of the court room opened and the judge made her way in.

"All rise …" said the court bailiff. "The honorable Judge Marion McIntyre is presiding."

"Be seated," said Judge Marion. She addressed the Plaintiff's lawyers first. "So, Ms. De Havilland is suing Ms. Monahan for negligence and abdication of responsibility as a school principal in keeping her building safe. Is this correct Mr. Markham?"

"Yes, your honour," he replied. "Ms. De Havilland is not seeking a cash settlement, but rather to have Ms. Monahan proven negligent and removed from her position as Principal of Viscount Elton School."

"I see," said Judge Marion, as she looked at the court documents on her bench. "Mr. Matishyn, you are legal counsel for Ms. Monahan, correct?"

"I am your honor," Darren replied.

"Alright then," Marion began, "This is not a typical trial obviously, nor is it a criminal trial. I am going to ask Mr. Markham to begin questioning. Who do you wish to call as your first witness?"

"We want to start with Ms. Monahan, your honour," said Markham.

"Very well," the judge said. "Ms. Monahan please come to the stand." Lianna stood up and walked to the witness stand and was sworn in by the bailiff. She was very nervous but tried to keep a smile on her face.

"Ms. Monahan," Markham began, "You are the administrator in charge of Viscount Elton School, correct?" He looked at Lianna with glaring eyes, trying to intimidate her.

"Yes," she responded calmly. She didn't want to appear nervous or intimidated by him.

"And you are ultimately responsible for what goes on in your building am I right?"

"Yes, but the school board has it's accountability when it comes to keeping the school in good repair," said Lianna. "They supervise caretakers etc. who clean the school. I let them know if things are not clean, but the caretakers let the facilities department know if things are broken or need fixing."

"So, the condition of the school is a shared responsibility then?" Markham asked.

"We each have our areas of responsibility. The condition of the building structure is not mine to fix. Only to inform if I see something that needs attention."

"And you let your caretaker know if anything needs repaired etc.?"

"Yes. I would let the caretaker know and he would submit a work order to have things repaired."

"So…it's your responsibility to inform the caretaker, who represents the facilities department," Markham clarified.

"Yes."

"Do you take regular walks through your building to examine its condition Ms. Monahan?" he asked.

"As often as I can. Schools are busy places and I rely on my caretaker to let me know about any problems, which are generally quite few."

"How often do you walk through the entire building, Ms. Monahan? Including the lower level or basement?" Lianna knew where Markham was going with this questioning and he was trying to trap her.

"As frequently as time allows. My caretaker does a safety walk around the building daily, which includes the exterior and all areas that children can access. He is thorough and I trust him."

"But how often do YOU personally walk through the building to check on things?" he asked Lianna again. "Once per day, once per week, once per month, once per year? Which is it?" Markham persisted.

"I can't give you the exact frequency," she replied. "I do my due diligence."

"Not according to Ms. De Havilland," Markham said, "because she has evidence that there are areas of the school which still contain hazardous materials and are accessible to students.

Your honour, I'd like to enter this report into evidence to show that issues existed with the building and also a copy of the email that was sent to Ms. Monahan informing her of the problem."

"All that information is compiled by the facilities department, Mr. Markham. I believe you already know that," Lianna reminded him.

"Indeed, you are right, Ms. Monahan. But are you not also accountable to review that information regularly?" he dug deeper.

"Those records are not stored at the school," Lianna said. "I get emailed a copy for our records and I'm sure it's in my archives. I look at it briefly, but I trust facilities to do their due diligence and ensure a safe building for us at the school."

"What if I told you that a certain report indicated areas that needed attention. Would it not be prudent for you to follow up on those recommendations?" Markham asked.

"I am only copied on those emails as a courtesy. Facilities are ultimately responsible for any required safety issues or risks," Lianna reminded him.

"But YOU are responsible for the safety of your staff and students, correct? I think that's what you said earlier." Markham was using her words against her and she didn't appreciate it.

"Objection your honour," said Darren. "Mr. Markham is implying culpability in his questioning and using her words against her."

"I'll allow the question," said Judge Marion.

"So, *you* are personally responsible for the safety of the students and staff in the building then," Markham stated, looking directly at Lianna. "And if there was a problem that you knew about, and didn't follow up with your caretaker to see if it was fixed, wouldn't that be neglecting your responsibility for ensuring safety?" Lianna was now getting angry and was going to push back.

"I did my due diligence, Mr. Markham. My caretaker also gets copies of the reports," Lianna answered.

Suddenly Judge Marion said, "Please answer the original question, Ms. Monahan."

Lianna was quiet and looked at Darren across the room. He nodded at her and she finally spoke. "I am responsible for acting on lawful orders of the Board. I was not instructed to take action on anything from the report you are speaking about. If I was asked to do something, I would have."

"I see you and I have a different definition of responsibility Ms. Monahan, and I can see you are clearly denying any responsibility for acting on the information that showed there were risks. No further questions your honour." Markham walked away from the witness stand and back to his seat with Noella.

"Mr. Matishyn ... your witness," said the judge.

Darren approached the witness stand and smiled at Lianna. "Ms. Monahan, you are well versed in all regulations of the Board am I right?"

"I am for sure! I regularly consult the policy manual as well if there is any doubt in my mind. I know the regulations and I adhere to all of them," Lianna started emphatically.

"You are probably well aware that the Facilities department is responsible for the upkeep and repair of the buildings in the system. What did you see in the report that came to you?" asked Darren.

"I'm glad you asked," said Lianna. "The report said that there were areas where exposure to asbestos was possible, but not likely. It also stated that there would be follow-up by Facilities to assess and mitigate the situation. I assumed that it would be taken care of, which is reasonable. In the end, I acted reasonably, which is the test of negligence in legal cases …

did the person act reasonably under the circumstances."

"I agree with you, Lianna, and the law seems to support you on that point," Darren said. "Can you please also tell the court about Ms. De Haviland's intrusions into meetings you were at, as well as her entry to the building when government inspectors were around."

Lianna proceeded to talk about Noella's erratic behaviour and how she barged into private meetings where she wasn't invited. Lianna testified about feeling threatened and unsafe, which she hoped would help her case.

Because Lianna knew Mitch Mason in the Facilities department, she knew about Noella's visit and the threats Noella made toward his career. But she also wondered whether Mitch might be somehow involved in this whole problem.

Lianna told the court about the vandalism to her property as well as Todd's tires and about the car that followed her on a couple of occasions. She talked about the break in at her condo and the way she and her family felt unsafe. The judge allowed her testimony to continue as she felt it was all relevant to Lianna's experience leading up to the trial.

"No further questions at this time your honor, said Darren.

"Thank you, Ms. Monahan," said the judge. "You may step down now." Lianna exited the witness stand and walked back to sit with Darren.

"Good job, Lianna," Darren whispered as she sat down beside him.

"Mr. Markham, do you wish to call another witness to the stand?" said the judge.

"Yes, I'd like to call Noella De Havilland your honour," said Markham.

Noella rose from her place and went toward the stand. The bailiff swore her in and she prepared for questions. "Hello Noella," Markham said. "Can you please tell us why we are here today?"

"Absolutely!" Noella began. "Ms. Monahan blatantly disregarded her responsibility to ensure a safe environment for my children … for all children … at Carlton. She is negligent and needs to be removed from her position." Noella spoke passionately and expanded on her reasoning regarding Lianna and the report she entered into evidence.

"When did you first discover there was a problem, Ms. De Havilland?" Markham asked her. "Soon after our last council meeting when I was walking through the school," Noella began. "I went downstairs and noticed some pipe covers were frayed and some of the ceiling tiles had been damaged.

It made me think about things I'd heard about construction of these old buildings. And by the way, when I went to take a drink from the fountain at the bottom of the stairs, the water was discolored and tasted horrible.

That's also when I decided to look into the purity of the water that students … including my children …were drinking on a daily basis. I decided to talk with the facilities department so I set up a meeting with Mitch Mason."

"I see, Noella. You became concerned about the safety of the building and what students could potentially be exposed to. Am I right?"

"For sure! I had to do something to prevent risk to the students - and the staff as well!"

"Sounds like you had the school's best interest in mind when you pursued this investigation, Noella."

"Indeed, I did," and she stared with contempt at Lianna from a distance.

"Objection!" said Darren. "Mr. Markham is speculating about the state of mind and intent of the plaintiff."

"Sustained," said Judge Marion, "Mr. Markham please refrain from making comments about Ms. De Haviland's intent.

"Thank you, your honour," said Darren.

Noella glared with even more intensity at Lianna who just smiled back across the room. Lianna was glad she had Darren in her corner, but she wondered what Noella would pull next.

"In your opinion, Noella," said Markham, "Did Ms. Monahan disregard the information in the facilities report?"

"Yes, she most definitely did," said Noella. "And now she has to answer for it! Mr. Mason was clear when he told me she had access to it."

"Thank you, Noella." said Markham. "No further questions for this witness your honour."

Noella stepped down and made her way back to the seat with her lawyer. She was confident that she would win this litigation and that Lianna would be removed.

"Just a minute, Ms. De Havilland," said Darren. "Your honour, we would like to cross examine here."

"Absolutely," said the judge. "Ms. De Haviland please return to the witness stand." Lianna now knew Darren was going to go after Noella and she couldn't wait to see how.

Chapter 32

Noella took her place on the witness stand and was looking somewhat nervous. She had a habit of flipping her hair with her hand when she was under pressure and now was no different. Every minute or so, she flipped her hair to the side and when she did, she tilted her head slightly in that direction.

"Ms. De Haviland, you were a city councilor a few years ago, correct?" asked Darren, who began a very direct line of questioning.

"That's right," she replied, looking confused about why he would ask. "How is this relevant to my case?"

"And you had a considerable power and influence when on city council am I correct?" Noella looked even more confused as he went on.

"I would say so yes, I did. Again, I'm not sure why that's relevant here."

"And your ex-husband, Collin … he is a successful businessman is he not?"

"Yes," she replied. Noella continued to glare at Lianna, who was also wondering where Darren would take this.

"Would it be fair to say that you had a strong connection to the business community when you were a city councilor then?" Darren asked.

"I wouldn't say it was anything unusual," Noella replied. "I knew many business people partly through my husband's business and his prominence in the community."

"Please establish some relevance here, Mr. Matishyn," said the judge suddenly.

"I will shortly, your honour," said Darren. He paused for a brief moment to consider his next question. "Your children go to Viscount Elton School am I right?"

"Yes," she said.

"And you are on the school council ... Vice Chair I believe?" Darren asked, now moving toward the relevance of his questioning.

"I am," Noella replied. She began to look a little nervous, and again began to flip her hair.

"And would it be fair to say that you were upset with Ms. Monahan for urging the council not to buy equipment for fine arts productions in the school?"

"I suppose so." Noella replied.

"And didn't you also storm out of the meeting when your proposal was rejected by council?"

"I wouldn't call it stormed," Noella responded.

"And you've been upset with Ms. Monahan since then, am I right?" Darren pointedly asked her.

"I suppose I have," she replied, flipping her hair with her left hand.

"Upset enough that you would look for reasons to have Ms. Monahan dismissed from her position? Upset enough that you would initiate an investigation about the school that would harm Ms. Monahan's reputation?" Darren asked.

"I am trying to protect my kids here," Noella said. "Ms. Monahan disregarded important safety information that would impact all children and staff in the school. The health department also did water testing and found lead in it … from the old pipes that should have been replaced."

"How did you have any idea that there were potential problems, Ms. De Haviland? You must have had some inside information from somewhere?"

"I don't know what you're talking about Mr. Matishyn."

"Did you, or did you not call one of the contractors who did renovation work on Carlton school a couple of years ago?" Darren asked her. "Bridgestone construction, I believe?"

"I called them about a matter involving my husband, who owns the company, yes." She now looked even more nervous than before.

"And in a side conversation, you discussed the Carlton building, am I right?"

"It may have been mentioned, yes."

"Ms. De Haviland, do you know Dave Monahan, Lianna's ex-husband?"

"We've met." She replied.

"Do you know Dave now works for Bridgestone?" Darren asked, knowing full well that Noella could not deny the connection.

"Lots of people work for Bridgestone," said Noella. "I can't keep up with them all."

"True," said Darren, "but you also had a conversation with Dave two weeks ago Monday, at 10:30 AM did you not?"

Noella knew Darren had done his homework and couldn't lie under oath. "Yes, I spoke with him," Noella said.

"And that's how you found out that Carlton had asbestos containing materials in the building, correct?"

"Dave may have mentioned that, yes." said Noella.

"Thank you, Ms. De Haviland, that's all my questions for now." Darren said and he looked at Lianna who gave him a thumbs up sign.

"Your honour, I'd like to call Dave Monahan to the witness stand please," Darren said firmly and with confidence. Dave had been sitting in the back of the court room, without Lianna knowing he was there. He made his way to the witness stand and was sworn in by the bailiff.

"Hello Mr. Monahan," said Darren. "I'm glad you could make it today.

"Objection, your honour," said Noella's lawyer Markham. "We were not notified of this witness and they weren't on the list."

"Your honour," said Darren, "I sent an email to Mr. Markham yesterday informing him that I'd be calling Mr. Monahan to the stand. I believe I have disclosed our intent within the acceptable guidelines and procedures."

"I'll allow the witness to be questioned. Mr. Markham you need to keep up with your email messages," said the judge.

"Mr. Monahan, do you own a blue car?" asked Darren.

"I do, but I don't drive it very often," Dave replied.

"And it's a Honda Civic, correct?" said Darren

"Yes. But I haven't driven it for a long time. It's been sitting in my garage for months," said Dave.

"That's interesting," said Darren, because your neighbors say that they've seen you driving it a few times in the past two weeks.

"They must have been mistaken then," said Dave.

"On the contrary Mr. Monahan," said Darren, "are you sure you don't want to change your answer to that question?"

"Why would I?" asked Dave, looking nervous as hell now.

Darren opened his computer to project video footage of Dave's car parked across the street from Lianna's condo. "Is that your car, Dave?" he asked him forcefully. "This was two nights ago, so again I ask if you'd like to change your answer."

"I loaned the car to a friend. I haven't driven it myself," answered Dave who was now backtracking.

"But you just told the court it was in your garage for months, Dave! So, you lied to the court!" said Darren emphatically.

"Objection!" said Markham. "He's badgering my client!"

"Overruled," said the judge. "But Mr. Matishyn, please establish the relevance of this to our case."

"Yes, your Honour," Darren replied. "Mr. Monahan, did you know that it was your car that was seen following Lianna's car on several occasions, and once very aggressively?

"No, I wasn't aware," said Dave. "Again, I haven't driven it in months."

Who did you loan the car to Mr. Monahan? Please tell the court."

Darren stared at Dave who finally and reluctantly gave an answer. "I loaned the car to Mitch Mason who works in the Facilities department for the school board." There was a murmur in the courtroom reacting to his answer.

"And let me guess ... you loaned your car to Mitch a couple of times in the past two weeks," said Darren, now becoming more direct with Dave.

"It's possible," said Dave as he shifted nervously on the witness stand.

"Possible," said Darren. "Is it also possible that you and Ms. De Haviland arranged to have Lianna followed by Mitch to intimidate her before the trial? And is it also possible that Mitch also broke into Lianna's condo, looking for a document?"

"That's ridiculous," said Dave. "Why would we have someone break into her place? What does she have that I would want?"

"It's not what you wanted, but what Ms. De Haviland wanted," said Darren. "You see Mr. Monahan, when Ms. De Haviland was in office, she took bribes from Bridgestone Construction, the company you work for and that's owned by her ex-husband.

She awarded contracts to that company, one of which was a tender to do asbestos abatement at Carlton School. That's how she found out about the asbestos and the two of you conspired to cover up the bribes. Am I correct?"

Dave was very nervous and knew that Lianna had some type of

evidence from the city. At that moment, he decided to come clean. He also thought about the hidden surveillance camera that Darren was well aware of and decided not to risk it coming out in court.

"Yes, you are right! Noella and I spoke!" responded Dave reluctantly. "She knew I was bitter about my marriage ending and so she took advantage of that. She asked me to have Lianna followed as well as find a way to get the evidence the city had against her. She offered money to have someone break into Lianna's condo and search for it. They found nothing."

"So, you found someone to follow your ex-wife Lianna and also break into her condo, is that correct?" Dave hesitated for a moment and told the court that Noella hired Mitch Mason who had worked as a caretaker in another school. Rumor has it that Lianna and Mitch had an affair, which Noella found out about. She was now blackmailing Mitch.

"Objection your honor!", said Markham. "Hearsay!"

"I'm going to allow this testimony Mr. Markham. Do you wish to cross examine the witness?"

"No, your honor" replied Markham.

"Mr. Matishyn, do you have any further questions?" asked the judge.

"Actually, your honor, the defense would like to call Mr. Todd Hackman to the stand."

"Objection, your honor!" said Markham. "This witness was also not on the list provided to us."

"Also listed in an email to Mr. Markham, your honor." Darren was pleased that Markham had also missed that email which took away more credibility for Noella.

Lianna was surprised by Darren's decision to put Todd on the stand, but she was convinced that it was for good reason. Todd came forward from the gallery and headed toward the witness stand. Lianna noticed that he looked very nervous, but he managed a smile as he passed by. The bailiff swore Todd in and soon the questioning began.

"Hello Mr. Hackman. Thank you for coming today, said Darren. "Can you please tell the court how you know Ms. Monahan?'

"We are both school principals, and currently in a relationship with each other." Todd looked at Lianna and smiled.

"I see, so you would consider the two of you very close and familiar with each other?"

"Yes, I would definitely say that," Todd answered.

"Mr. Hackman, can you tell us where you worked before you became a principal at your current school?" Darren asked him.

"Sure," Todd said. "I was a teacher at Mountain Valley as well as Senator Nigel Steele."

"I see," responded Darren. "Did you work with Mr. Mitch Mason at one of those schools?"

"As a matter of fact, yes. Mr. Mason was a caretaker at Mountain Valley School." Stated Todd.

"And did you in fact meet Ms. De Haviland while you worked at Mountain Valley?" Darren was now pushing the envelope of Lianna's defense and Lianna was getting nervous. Todd looked at her before he answered the question.

"Yes, that's true. Mr. Mason and Ms. De Haviland were often seen together after school ended each day. Some thought they were romantically involved." Todd thought his testimony would help Lianna's case.

"But Mr. Hackman, is it true that you also became involved with Ms. De Haviland soon after Mr. Mason and her broke up?" There was a loud murmur in the courtroom this time and Lianna reacted with a shocked look on her face. She wondered where Darren was going with this, but even more importantly, why had Todd never told her about Noella.

There was a long pause, and finally the judge turned to Todd and said, "Please answer the question, Mr. Hackman."

"It's true," said Todd and he looked down at his feet.

"Please tell the court about a phone conversation you had 2 weeks ago with Ms. De Haviland. I believe you spoke about Lianna's situation did you not?"

'We did, but I'm having trouble remembering all the details." Todd responded.

"Mr. Hackman, I have investigated this thoroughly and I can tell you she asked for information about Lianna. Not only that, she told you that if you cooperated with her plan, she would keep your relationship a secret from Lianna, as she knew Lianna would be upset. She also offered to pay you $2000 dollars for access to Lianna's condo building did she not?" Darren now knew this would be a problem for Lianna and that she and Todd would likely break up, but he had to expose the truth to build more evidence against

Lianna.

"I gave her the code to the building that she then passed on to others who could break into the unit. I'm so sorry Lianna ... I was being blackmailed by Noella and I couldn't let you find out about our past together." Todd began to shed tears on the stand, and Lianna just looked away, also shedding tears. She knew it was over.

"And did the person you gave the code to also install a secret camera to record audio and video inside her condo?"

"I'm not sure, but it is possible," Todd replied.

"Was it Noella who hired Mitch Mason to follow Lianna and break into her condo unit?" Darren asked Todd.

"I'm afraid so, yes," said Todd reluctantly.

"Your honor. I want to move for a dismissal of the accusations against Ms. Monahan," Darren began. "Obviously she was under duress in this situation and clearly Ms. De Haviland has broken the law. We wouldn't be here now if she hadn't. The Board was responsible for correcting the situation with the asbestos, and steps were taken by the Facilities department to begin reparations. Ms. Monahan acted reasonably in her capacity as Principal to protect students and staff. Therefore, I must ask you to rule for the defendant here."

"I agree with you, Mr. Matishyn. I will be ruling in favour of Ms. Monahan."

There was a cheer in the court room as many of Lianna's friend came to support her. "Furthermore ..." the judge began, I'm asking the bailiff to take Ms. De Haviland *and* Mr. Monahan into custody for questioning in this matter." The judge wrote some notes on a pad of paper in front of her.

"Ms. De Haviland ... you've demonstrated a disregard for due process of law as well as the audacity to accept bribes as a public official. You are also now connected to an indictable offence of breaking and entering and I have no tolerance for criminals in my court room. Especially when they are trying to bully innocent people. You have blackmailed Mr. Hackman who has had a great reputation and turned Mr. Mason into a common criminal. With that said ... Bailiff ...please remove these two people immediately!"

The bailiff first went to get Noella from the lawyers' desk where Markham was looking dumbfounded. Noella glared at Lianna as the bailiff walked her over to the front of the court room where the door leading to remand was located. As he passed the stand, he grabbed Dave by the arm and also escorted him and Noella out the door and down the hallway to police questioning.

"I'm also issuing a warrant for the arrest of Mr. Mason. Mr. Hackman, there is no precedent for charges or conviction for giving out a security code. You're obviously going to pay for these actions for some time to come. You've actually punished yourself in this situation. Case dismissed!" proclaimed Judge Marion as she pounded her gavel on the bench.

Naturally, Lianna was relieved at the verdict, and she emphatically thanked Darren for his efforts and excellent work. Her children came to give her a hug immediately, and together they walked out knowing they needn't worry about Noella ever again.

Chapter 33

The next few weeks went smoothly for Lianna. She returned to work a few days after the trial with the joyful reception of her staff but was devastated over losing Todd. She had the sympathy of all her colleagues who were sure Todd was the right one for her.

There were balloons everywhere in the staff room as well as plenty of treats and sweets to get everyone through the day. Patricia was especially happy to see Lianna back at work and gave her a hug that seemed to last forever. "So good you are back, Ms. Lianna. I missed you dearly!"

Lianna was touched by this sentimental expression of emotion and admiration. "Thank you, Patricia! It's great to be back!"

Patricia looked at Lianna once again and in a whisper, said to her, "I heard Ms. De Haviland might be spending some time behind bars." She looked for Lianna's reaction and her thoughts were confirmed.

"That's true Patricia, but we will have to wait and see."

"I'm not sorry she was caught," said Patricia, who really didn't like Noella at all. "I just can't figure out why she wanted to ruin your career." Patricia looked at Lianna with understanding and sympathy.

A week went by and Lianna was still lamenting about how things turned out with Todd. She decided to take her girls out to a fancy dinner up the tower with a revolving restaurant overlooking the entire city, hoping that would make her feel happier. The views were nothing short of breathtaking, and the mood was relaxed but the conversation gradually turned to the events of the past 2 weeks with Noella. The girls wanted to focus on Lianna's strength throughout the ordeal.

"Noella found out about the asbestos, then decided to go after you by saying you ignored it?" Diane asked.

"Yes, dear. That's the way it happened. She was angry about the money I wouldn't commit to the fine arts program and she wanted to get even. She's used to getting her way, and so she had to do it one way or another."

"And Dad was involved in following you, or at least having someone do it, right mom?" Dallas asked.

"I'm afraid so dear. Noella pressured him into having someone use his car, which I didn't recognize because he bought it after we split up," Lianna replied. "But the bigger disappointment was that Todd and Noella had an affair a few years ago, which he didn't tell me about. Noella blackmailed him into giving her the code to our building and she passed it on. She threatened to tell me about their affair and he couldn't bear losing me. Not only that, she was blackmailing another former lover of hers who works for the school board. Mitch Mason, who also had an affair with her, was the one who she pressured into following me … using Dad's car! We think it was Mitch who broke into our apartment."

"Unbelievable!" said Diane, who was absolutely shocked by this news.

"So now, there is an arrest warrant for Mitch, and Noella has been taken into custody. Dad may be charged for his involvement, but we're not sure how that's going to turn out."

"I'm sorry you two girls had to go through all this. It wasn't pleasant and your dad had no regard for your feelings." Lianna continued to tell them about the hidden camera in the picture frame and that sent them over the edge. "The hidden camera allowed him to know when we were coming and going from the condo so he could follow me. He also knew when it was a good time to break into the condo."

"That scumbag!" said Diane. "That is just sick!"

"Unbelievable," said Dallas. "Can we ever trust Dad again? Even if he is cleared of any charges, he was responsible for the video footage that helped Noella plan the break in."

"That's true," said Lianna. "I have mixed feelings about that, as Noella did pressure him into it.

"I can't believe that they could trace where the video was being streamed to," said Diane. "Modern technology can be a blessing but also a curse!"

They sat for about an hour after dinner reminiscing about old times together and being grateful that they had each other for support.

"There's still something I need to know," said Diane. How did Noella know there was someone at the city offices who knew she accepted bribes?"

"Well," said Lianna, "it turns out that Dad was so angry with Noella at that he decided to inform the contracts department about Noella's indiscretions. He stole company information to prove that Noella had been paid and he gave that to the city staff … the very information that brought Noella down."

"So, Dad was both her ally and her enemy in the end," said Dallas.

"You're so smart sweetheart. Maybe you should become an investigator of some kind. Maybe a forensic one, or maybe a detective?"

Lianna teased.

"Oh, Mom!" said Dallas. "You know I want to become a school principal just like you!" Dallas said facetiously. "But without all the drama!" They all laughed as they finished their desserts and then headed back home. The rest of the evening was spent playing board games and telling jokes which brought them all closer together.

Suddenly, Lianna's cell phone rang. She answered it carefully. "Hello? Yes, this is Lianna Monahan." There were a few seconds of silence then a very horrified look came to Lianna's face.

"Thanks for letting me know" she said in a worried tone of voice. She ended the call and sat back in her chair, almost stunned by the news. "That was the Police," she said. "Noella has been released on bail but is nowhere to be found."

This is a purely fictional story. All the names, characters, places, events and incidents in this book are the product of the author's imagination and used in a fictitious manner. Any resemblance to actual persons, living or dead, or actual events or places is purely coincidental.

Manufactured by Amazon.ca
Acheson, AB

14614020R00140